USAREUR

USAREUR

The United States Army in Europe

Text and Photographs by Michael Skinner

Presidio Press ★ Novato, California
THE PRESIDIO POWER SERIES
LANDPOWER #3003

Published by Presidio Press
31 Pamaron Way, Novato, CA 94949

Library of Congress Cataloging-in-Publication Data

Skinner, Michael, 1953–
    USAREUR: the United States Army in Europe.

    (The Presidio power series.   Landpower; #3003)
    1. United States.   Armed Forces—Europe.   2. United
States.   Army.   Europe and Seventh Army.   3. Europe—
Defenses.   I. Title.   II. Title: United States Army in
Europe.   III. Series.
UA26.E9S54   1989   355.3′1   88–25386
ISBN 0–89141–311–1

Photographs copyright © Michael Skinner, except:
pages 15, 35, 42, 44, 63, 87, 91, 108, 110 and 123, U.S. Army.

Michael Skinner uses Nikon cameras and lenses exclusively.

Printed by Singapore National Printer, coordinated by Palace Press.

Contents

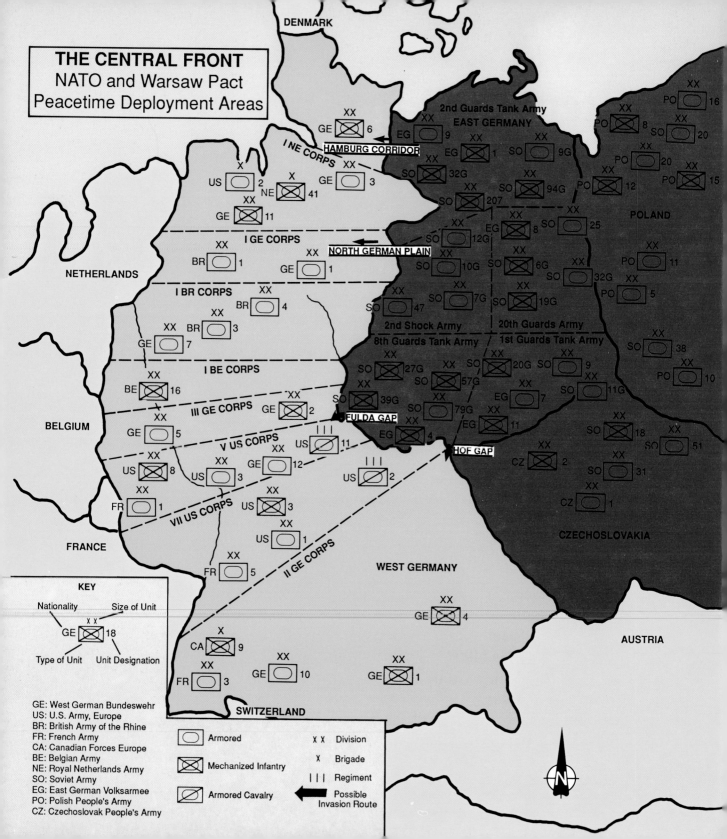

THE CENTRAL FRONT
NATO and Warsaw Pact
Peacetime Deployment Areas

DENMARK

GE XX 6
I NE CORPS
← HAMBURG CORRIDOR

2nd Guards Tank Army
EAST GERMANY

EG 9
EG XX 1   SO 9G
SO 32G
SO 207

US 2   X NE XX 41
GE XX 3

GE XX 11

I GE CORPS
← NORTH GERMAN PLAIN

SO XX 8   SO 25
PO XX 12   PO 20   PO 15
PO XX 16   SO 20

POLAND

NETHERLANDS

BR 1   GE 1

I BR CORPS

BR XX 4

GE XX 7   BR XX 3

I BE CORPS

BELGIUM

BE XX 16

III GE CORPS   GE XX 2

GE 5

V US CORPS   US ⊘ 11

US XX 8   US 3   GE 12

FR 1   VII US CORPS   US XX 3

US 1

FR XX 5   II GE CORPS

FRANCE

KEY

Nationality   Size of Unit

GE XX 18

Type of Unit   Unit Designation

GE: West German Bundeswehr
US: U.S. Army, Europe
BR: British Army of the Rhine
FR: French Army
CA: Canadian Forces Europe
BE: Belgian Army
NE: Royal Netherlands Army
SO: Soviet Army
EG: East German Volksarmee
PO: Polish People's Army
CZ: Czechoslovak People's Army

EG XX 12G   SO 8
SO XX 10G   SO 6G   SO 32G
SO 7G   SO XX 19G
SO 47

2nd Shock Army   20th Guards Army
8th Guards Tank Army   1st Guards Tank Army

SO XX 27G   SO XX 20G   SO 9
SO XX 57G   EG 7   SO 11G
SO XX 39G   SO 79G
← FULDA GAP   EG XX 11
EG 4
HOF GAP →   CZ XX 2

SO XX 38
PO 10

SO XX 18
SO 51

SO 31

CZ 1

CZECHOSLOVAKIA

US ⊘ 2

WEST GERMANY

GE XX 4

FR XX 5

AUSTRIA

CA X 9

FR XX 3   GE 10   GE XX 1

SWITZERLAND

Armored   XX Division
Mechanized Infantry   X Brigade
Regiment ⫴   ⫴ Regiment
Armored Cavalry   ◄ Possible Invasion Route

N

USAREUR Maneuver Units In Central Germany

BORDER CAMPS and OBSERVATION POST

① O.P. India 3/11 ACR
② O.P. Romeo 3/11 ACR
③ O.P. Alpha 1/11 ACR
④ O.P. Tennessee 2/11 ACR
⑤ Camp Lee 2/11 ACR
⑥ Camp Harris 4-4 Cav / 3 AD
⑦ Camp Hof 2/2 ACR
⑧ Camp Gates 1/2 ACR
⑨ Camp Pitman 1-1 Cav / 1 AD
⑩ Camp Reed 3/2 ACR
⑪ Camp May 3/2 ACR

HANNOVER

COLOGNE

BONN

Rhine

Bad Hersfeld ③

Giessen

Fulda ④

Kirchgoens
Friedberg ⑤

Budingen ⑥ ⑦
Geinhausen
Hanau   Bad Kissingen
FRANKFURT
Aschaffenburg   Schweinfurt   Bayreuth
Mainz
Babenhausen   Bamberg   ⑧
Bad Kreuznach   Darmstadt
Wurzburg   Grafenwohr Range ⑨
Wertheim   Kitzingen
Baumholder   Illesheim
Herzogendurach   Erlangen   Amberg
Kaiserslautern   Mannheim
Zirndorf   NUREMBERG   ⑩
Heidelberg   Schwabach   Hohenfels Range
                                      ⑪

Karlsruhe

STUTTGART   Schwabisch Gmund

Augsburg

MUNICH

N

Bad Tolz

Amberg: 3/2 ACR
Ansbach: HQ 1 AD
Aschaffenburg: 3/3 ID
Augsburg: 17 FA Bde
Babenhausen: 41 FA Bde
Bad Hersfeld: 3/11 ACR
Bad Kissngen: 2/11 ACR
Bad Kreuznach: HQ 8 ID
Bad Tolz: Det. A 1-10 Special Forces
Bamberg: 3/1 AD, 2/2 ACR
Baumholder: 2/8 ID, 8 ID DivArty
Bayreuth: 1/2 ACR
Budingen: 3-12 Cav / 3 AD
Darmstadt: HQ 32 ADCOM, 10 ADA Bde
Erlangen: 2/1 AD
Frankfurt: HQ US V Corps, HQ 3 AD, 4/3 AD, 130 Eng Bde
Friedberg: 3/3 AD
Fulda: HQ 11 ACR, 1/11 ACR, 4/11 ACR
Geinhausen: 2/3 AD

Giessen: 42 FA Bde
Hanau: 4/3 AD, 3 AD DivArty
Heidelberg: HQ SEVENTH US Army
Herzogendurach: 210 FA Bde
Illesheim: 1/1 AD, 4/1 AD
Kaiserslautern: 94 ADA Bde
Karlsruhe: 18 Eng Bde
Kirchgoens: 1/3 AD
Kitzingen: 3 ID DivArty, 2/3 ID, 4/3 ID
Mainz: 1/8 ID, 4/8 ID
Mannheim: 3/8 ID, 3-8 CAV / 8 ID
Nurnberg: HQ 2 ACR, 4/2 ACR
Schwabach: 1/1 CAV / 1 AD
Schwabisch Gmund: 56 FACOM
Schweinfurt: 1/3 ID, 3/7 CAV / 3 ID
Stuttgart: HQ US VII Corps, 7 Eng Bde
Westheim: 72 FA Bde
Wurzburg: HQ 3 ID, 69 ADA Bde
Zirndorf: 1 AD DivArty

Preface

There's a war outside the Tower Motel. Holed up inside, I've got everything I need: bad German food and worse German cable TV. Turn up the volume and you hardly notice the 155mm artillery shells rattling the thin windows, rolling like Texas thunder across the farm fields between the range and me.

You can try to ignore the booming, but you can't stop it. Grafenwohr is ground zero in the Central European cockpit. They've been pounding this particular piece of real estate for about a hundred years, popping off small arms, cranking the tanks, yanking the lanyards on main guns pointed east, west, north, south. It's a firing range. It's *supposed* to sound ominous.

From the balcony, day and night, you hear the war, the continuous war, the war between Us and Them, the good guys and the bad. This generation the players line up west and east: NATO, all hope and cavalry, pacing "the trace." On the other side of the cut, the Russians and their dim allies squat, leaning forward in their armored cynicism. You can't hear their guns from here, but I don't imagine they sound much different than ours.

Start anywhere you want—politics, history, the humanities—this is where you'll end up, listening for guns in the German night. It's the largest piece of unfinished business on the planet. Everything else is a peripheral theater.

In writing on this subject, I follow some pretty heavy hitters. There is no dearth of material concerning the military matchup in Central Europe, but most of it is abstract stuff, dealing with strategic questions. For hard answers on the operational and tactical level, there are none better than David Isby or Steve Zaloga. Isby's book *Armies of NATO's Central Front* (written with the equally capable Charles Kamps) is a good place to look for accurate detail on the subject. Zaloga is the best tank man in the business. And some of the sharper World War III pre-historians around are wargamers. Among the best: Frank Chadwick, Jim Dunnigan, and Stephen Patrick.

I read a number of U.S. Army manuals, none of which offered significant insight. Of much more use were a couple of semiofficial army magazines, *Armor* for tank and CAV tactics and *Aviation Digest* for helicopters. Speaking of helicopters, thanks to Lt. Col. Steve Rausch, Capt. Steve Huyett, Mr. Bill Hayes, and Mrs. Betty Goodson at Fort Rucker for a much closer look at army choppers than I could ever get in Europe.

The USAREUR tour was arranged by Lt. Col. Dave Burpee in the Pentagon and set up by Sgt. Elaine Venema at HQ Seventh Army. In one of the most impressive administrative feats I've seen in a long time of dealing with public affairs types, everything she promised came true and every stop in her ambitious schedule came off

---

Left: Only authorized American soldiers are allowed near the border.

ix

perfectly; I eventually ran out of things I could ask to do. Only the Army would have the good sense to trust enlisted personnel with this, but I think they should promote her to general and make her CINCEUR.

Special thanks to Joan Griffin, who edited this book, and Lynn Dragonette, who designed it. And ''tanks'' to the officers and men of the U.S. Army in Europe, who let me crank their tanks, walk their wires, and get a look at what it's really like on the line.

I came to Germany to get some answers. Tactically, I got some: I now know how to kill tanks, roast choppers, and pop caps with the best of them. Those answers are in this book. Strategically, I'm as uncertain as anyone in the White House or the Kremlin. Does there have to be another World War? Will we ever be able to live surely more than eighteen minutes into the future? Those answers, I'm afraid, are locked up in hearts armored too thickly for any weapon to penetrate.

Grafenwohr, West Germany
April, 1987

Lonely Huey takes off for another ash and trash mission over Bavaria.

Glossary

ACR: armored cavalry regiment

Active Defense: late 1970s development of NATO Forward Defense philosophy; rejected as unrealistic

AD: armored division

ADA: air defense artillery

AFV: armored fighting vehicle

AH-1: U.S. Army Cobra attack helicopter

AH-64: U.S. Army Apache attack helicopter

AirLand Battle: latest U.S. Army doctrine, stressing shock and maneuver over numbers and firepower

APC: armored personnel carrier

APFSDS-T: armor piercing fin stabilized discarding sabot–tungsten; main gun round for killing tanks

Area of Influence: AirLand Battle jargon for area occupied by enemy that will probably affect a unit's current operations

Area of Interest: AirLand Battle jargon for area occupied by enemy that could affect a unit's future operations

Army of Excellence (AOE): an early 1980s U.S. Army initiative culminating in a number of improvements, including the Army Studies 86 reorganization and the AirLand Battle doctrine

Army Studies 86: a U.S. Army analysis to determine the optimum organization of combat units; studies included Light Division 86, Heavy Division 86, Corps 86, and Echelon Above Corps 86

AWLS: amber warning light system; safety beacon required by West German government on all tracked vehicles

B horse: slang for Blackhorse, nickname of the 11th ACR

BAOR: British Army of the Rhine

BDU: battle dress utilities; standard U.S. Army fieldwear

BFV: Bradley fighting vehicle; the M2 and M3

BGS: Bundesgrenzschutz; West German paramilitary law enforcement organization

BMP: principal Soviet IFV

BTR: principal Soviet APC

Bundeswehr: Army of the Federal Republic of Germany

CBW: chemical/biological warfare; "bugs and gas"

Chobham armor: advanced ceramic laminate tank armor, designed at British research facility in Chobham, Surrey

COHORT: cohesion, operational readiness, and training; U.S. Army program to develop unit continuity

covering force: AirLand Battle term for units screening enemy while allied units move or regroup

CUC-V: commercial utility cargo vehicle; American production trucks and four-wheel-drive vehicles used for light duty

CVC: combat vehicle, crewman; U.S. Army tanker's helmet

Division 86: U.S. Army divisional reorganization plan

Dragon: standard U.S. Army medium antitank missile

Dragoons: nickname for 2d ACR

DU: depleted uranium; used in tank round penetrator

FAAS-V: field artillery ammunition support vehicle; new U.S. Army tracked ammunition carrier and loader

FEBA: forward edge of battle area; line of contact between opposing ground forces

First Battle: U.S. Army wargame simulating opening stages of general European war

Forward Defense: NATO doctrine entailing stopping an invasion as close to the border as possible

FTX: field training exercise

Fulda Gap: potential invasion route to Frankfurt

GAK: Grenze Aufklener; trusted East German Border Command guards

GDP: general deployment positions; "real world" battle positions that USAREUR units in garrison would occupy during initial attack

HEMTT: heavy expanded mobility tactical truck; new U.S. Army prime mover

Hind: Mi-24, principal Soviet attack helicopter

HMMW-V: high mobility, multipurpose wheeled vehicle; high-tech jeep replacement, sometimes called "Hummer" in the press, but referred to by soldiers as the "Hum-Vee"

Hof Gap: potential invasion route to Bavaria

Hydra 70: computer-controlled rocket system for AH-1

ICM: U.S. Army infantryman's flak vest

IFV: infantry fighting vehicle

IPB: Intelligence preparation of the battlefield

Ironland: nickname for 1st AD garrison positions in Bavaria

JAAT: joint air attack team; doctrine for coordinated attack by U.S. Air Force aircraft and U.S. Army helicopters and artillery

Kevlar: trade name for a type of lightweight armor

LAW: light antitank weapon; M72 one-shot rocket launcher

LBE: load bearing equipment; web gear used to hold infantryman's equipment

LD: line of departure

LHX: light helicopter, experimental; U.S. Army requirement for a new family of scout and utility helicopters

LZ: landing zone

MBA: main battle area; although it has a highly specific definition in AirLand Battle doctrine, this is essentially the battlefield

MBT: main battle tank

MBT-70: joint U.S.–West German project to design a common main battle tank; eventually abandoned

Meiningen Gap: a narrow offshoot of the Fulda Gap

MERDC: Mobility Equipment Research and Development Command; U.S. Army agency at Fort Belvoir, Va., responsible for designing tactical camouflage for American AFVs

METT: mission, enemy, terrain, time; basic requirements of an operational order; sometimes an extra "T" is appended, for troops available

MILES: multiple integrated laser engagement system; low-power laser projectors and detectors used to simulate combat in exercises

MOPP: mission-oriented protective posture; defense against chemical attack; various MOPP levels determine the degree of MOPP gear

Mr. Deuce: nickname for M2 HB .50-caliber heavy machine gun

MRE: meal, ready to eat; new U.S. Army combat rations

M1: Abrams main battle tank

M2: Bradley infantry fighting vehicle

M3: cavalry version of M2; formerly called Deavers cavalry fighting vehicle

M9: new U.S. Army bayonet

M48: Chapparal tracked infrared surface-to-air missile system

M60: former U.S. Army main battle tank; M60A3 is the latest version

M63: Vulcan tracked 20mm air defense gun

M109: 155mm self-propelled gun; standard artillery piece of U.S. Army and most NATO nations

M110: self-propelled 203mm howitzer; primary counterbattery artillery piece of U.S. Army and many NATO countries

M113: standard U.S. Army APC

M551: Sheridan light tank

M577: mobile command post based on M113 chassis

M1973: Soviet 152mm self-propelled gun

M1974: Soviet 122mm self-propelled gun

NADGE: NATO Air Defense Ground Environment; network of radars and command centers

NATO: North Atlantic Treaty Organization

NOE: nap of the earth

OH-58: Kiowa scout helicopter

OMG: operational maneuver group; new Soviet concept of an armor-heavy task force to exploit breakthroughs

POV: personally owned vehicle

POW: personally owned weapon

PRC-77: U.S. Army standard battlefield radio; pronounced ''Prick 77''

PW: prisoner of war

Reforger: return of forces to Germany; annual USAREUR deployment exercise integrating reinforcements from the United States; usually conducted with a related field training exercise

RISE: reliability improvement of selected equipment; upgrade program for M60A1

RPG: rocket-propelled grenade

sabot: metal collar attached to penetrator in main gun round to grip barrel and impart greater energy; discarded in flight (pronounced ''SAY–bo'')

SAM: surface-to-air missile

Seventh Army: parent organization for USAREUR units; HQ Heidelberg

shaped charge: chemical warhead using tremendous heat and pressure to penetrate armor; used on most antitank guided weapons, said to be virtually ineffective against Chobham armor

staballoy: U.S. Army euphemism for tank rounds made of depleted uranium

TACFIRE: U.S. Army artillery fire direction system

TADS: target acquisition and designation sight; fire-control system aboard AH-64 Apache attack helicopter

TC: tank commander

Three Sisters: area near Fulda on the inner German border dominated by six hills

TOW: tube-launched, optically tracked, wire-guided; U.S. Army BGM-71 heavy antitank missile

treadheads: derisive nickname hung on armor soldiers by infantrymen

tripwire: obsolete NATO strategy implying an early resort to nuclear weapons

UH-1: U.S. Army Iroquois utility helicopter; better known as the ''Huey''

V Corps: NATO V U.S. Corps; USAREUR units based in the Frankfurt area

VII Corps: NATO VII U.S. Corps; USAREUR units based in Bavaria

web gear: soldier's term for load bearing equipment

ZA: zone of attack

The Trace

On April 25, 1945, Soviet and American troops met and shook hands, perhaps for the last time, at Torgau, about sixty miles south of Berlin. Roads and bridges into Soviet-occupied Germany were blocked two weeks later. The victorious Western armies withdrew into their zones of occupation, determined long before the end of the war. Germany, meant to be temporarily divided into four parts, was permanently divided into two. A pencil mark on a map, drawn more or less casually by war-weary allies, trusting and naive, became a bayonet scar dragged through the ashes of Germany. And we've been staring at each other across that line ever since.

It is an imaginary line drawn across the heart of Europe, splitting Germany, and the world, ideologically and militarily. The greatest armies the earth has ever known — could ever know — are facing off there, ready to torch the planet over what is, essentially, a 700-mile-long scratch in the dirt.

Unlike most national borders, no natural barriers separate East and West Germany. Except for a brief stretch of the Elbe near Hamburg and some rough country to the south, there are no great rivers or mountain ranges to deter invasion; only politics divides what has become the German Democratic Republic and the Federal Republic of Germany (FRG).

Seen from the West, Churchill's Iron Curtain has devolved into a steel grill forged of Soviet iron and the blackened carbon of once-independent Eastern European nations. A pair of high metal fences marks the frontier of the German Democratic Republic and the limits of the Free World. The inside fence is electrified with a six-volt charge — just enough juice to send a signal to East German Border Command guards keeping the watch in concrete minarets. The mines that used to line their side of the border have been removed. Although the East German government tried to make propaganda capital out of the removal, the truth is the command-detonated mines were unpredictable and perhaps more dangerous to innocent bystanders, Border Command guards, and stray livestock than they were to escapees.

From the East, the border is considered, as is the Berlin Wall, an "anti-Fascist protective barrier," a prophylactic against resurgent Nazism and the decadent lure of the materialistic West. They work hard to keep the cultures apart. Behind the barrier at the frontier, there's a "hinterland" fence as much as three miles back from the line. The Border Command has also erected an anti-vehicle ditch just inside the border fence to "help deter invasion." Closer examination reveals the barrier is facing the wrong way to do that. At any rate, the barrier wouldn't stop a tank, but it would surely prevent any East German from driving through the fence in a car.

To the governments of the two Germanies, the "inner German border" (IGB) is, officially, no big deal. Legally, the Federal Republic of Germany and the German Democratic Republic consider the IGB no more formidable than a state line, say, or the boundary between two provinces. In theory, citizens of both countries can go freely back and forth, with just a short check at any number of "blue" autobahn crossings. In practice the border is only semipermeable.

But to the officers and men of the United States Army in Europe, who are pledged to shed their

2

CO of Camp Gates, a border outpost run by 1st Squadron, 2d ACR. The AWLS (amber warning light system) is required on all military vehicles by West German law.

lives for this intellectual construction, the border is known simply as "the trace." It is one of those rare, perfectly suited military terms, evoking, as it does, images of range wars, cavalry sorties from frontier outposts, and long riders, lonely, cold, and ever watchful, checking stretches of wire in a dulling and dangerous routine. That's life on the border today.

For more than forty years, USAREUR troops, the British Army of the Rhine, the resurgent Bundeswehr, the reluctant French, and resentful allies have been keeping a wary eye to the east.

Through moods alternating between neglect and paranoia, NATO strives to keep the unfinished business of World War II from combusting into World War III. It is a bad peace, but the most peace Central Europe has ever known.

For USAREUR, as it is with most NATO allies, the trace is cavalry country. To the north, along the famous Fulda Gap, the equally famous

Blackhorse Cav of the 11th Armored Cavalry Regiment (ACR) is strung out along a series of outposts. The Regiment's 3d Squadron mans two observation posts, India and Romeo, on the border north of its headquarters in Bad Hersfeld. The 2d Squadron, stationed in Bad Kissengen, operates a border camp, Camp Lee, cycling in a complete troop or tank company a month at a time to keep an eye on the Meiningen Gap. They keep two vehicles and crews at their observation post, called "Tennessee" in honor of a Blackhorse trooper nicknamed Tennessee, who was killed in Vietnam. The regiment's first squadron deploys platoon-sized elements from its base at Fulda to its observation post, "Alfa," right on the border at Rasdorf.

To the south and Czechoslovakia, the 2d Armored Cavalry Regiment keeps watch from a series of base camps near the border. The Dragoons are rich in tradition. Starting out in 1836 as the 2d Regimental Dragoons (Heavy Cavalry), they are the oldest continuously serving cavalry unit in the U.S. Army. The Dragoons have their own museum at Merrill Barracks — their headquarters in Nuremberg — which used to house Hitler's SS troopers during the prewar Nazi rallies. Until a couple of years ago, the entranceway was still scarred with automatic weapons fire.

The 2d ACR's sector is nearly twice as long as the Blackhorse's, and spans two borders. So the Dragoons rely on a half-dozen base camps strung along their 400-mile section of the trace. Camp Hof, Camp Gates, Camp Reed, and Camp May are run by the three squadrons of the 2d ACR. The other two — Camp Harris and Camp Pittman — are manned by the divisional cavalry squadrons of USAREUR's armored divisions. Entire cav troops or tank companies — about 130 men — are stationed at the border camps. At any given time, a third of the regiment, the equivalent of an entire cav squadron, is out on the line.

Although they have long since traded their horses for main battle tanks and armored personnel carriers (the Dragoons, those diehards, gave up theirs only reluctantly in 1942), there's still a lot of cavalry in the cav. Soldiers (called troopers) don't just get in and crank the tank, they "saddle up" or "mount up." Maintenance, or "taking care of the horse," as it's called, is done before the troops chow down. They still hold regimental balls, where officers wear spurs with their dress uniforms, although the tradition of forcing newcomers to drink beer from a riding boot has been outlawed in the light of Action Army regulations.

"Cavalry is not an organization you belong to. It's a state of mind," says a Blackhorse officer. "You get soldiers who don't normally get to serve in the cavalry — clerks, mechanics, people like that — once they get into the cav, they get a different mentality about doing things. Most of them have the mentality that there's no such thing as 'no' or 'can't do it.' The primary reason is that we do have a mission. We're constantly on the go here. Nothing ever stops."

That mission is patrolling the border. Every day, like grizzled horse soldiers, troopers of the armored cavalry squadrons mount up and "pace the trace." Typically, two platoons, one tank and one scout, form a mission reaction team at the border camp. From these come the daily patrols: four troopers and a noncommissioned officer. They leave their heavy hardware behind and troll the border in a pair of jeeps. A small, armored "ready force" of tanks and APCs is kept

2d ACR "Redcatcher" flight scrambles to "pace the trace."

Specially trained multilingual officers ride shotgun aboard every border patrol flight.

on alert at base camps, in case more firepower is quickly needed.

The cav also rides the trace in helicopters — OH-58 scout ships and AH-1 gunships mainly, although Hueys and Blackhawks are used occasionally. Border pilots are chosen for their judgement as much as their flying skills. They undergo a rigorous training schedule and are required to learn their section of the border by heart.

The Cobras carry no weapons save the gun, and even that is unloaded. The Americans aren't there to start trouble. There is great premium put on not appearing too warlike at the jumping off point for World War III. Troopers brandish no weapons on the border. Officers wear side-arms, but one gets the impression they are not loaded. Only specially trained troopers are al-

lowed near the trace. Regular American soldiers must stay outside the restricted zone, a kilometer back from the border, lest they stray across the irregular and often poorly marked line.

For their part, the Soviets and their Warsaw Pact allies also keep a low profile. Like the cav, Warsaw Pact forces maintain border camps, conduct dismounted patrols, and occupy observation posts. But there are no great armies lined up muzzle to muzzle across the inner German border, as one might suspect. In inclement weather, that is to say, most of the time, there are few people visible on either side of the fence. That doesn't mean there's no one out there. A cast of thousands, on both sides of the line, is keeping an eye out for its interests.

You might spy the odd Russian squad skulking

M3 cavalry fighting vehicle of the 11th ACR. The Black-horse Cav has been watching the border since its return from Vietnam.

along the East German fence in a GAZ-69 jeep, but ordinarily the Soviets are farther back, in garrison. They leave the day-to-day patrols to the East German Border Command (BC), a para-military force equipped with armored cars and light infantry weapons. Only the most trusted BC officers, the Grenze Aufklener or GAKs, as they are called, are allowed on the western side of the fence. Many take that opportunity to escape to West Germany.

To the south, the Czechoslovakian Pioneer Service (PS) performs police roles along their border with West Germany. The PS is considered less professional and more aggressive than the East German BC. Their border is less well delineated, with most barriers set far back from the national boundary itself. While much of the

line is a ''wet border'' — marked by small streams and rivers — a large section is indicated only by small white posts.

The confusion, coupled with aggression, has led to some nasty incidents. While chasing a Czech fugitive in 1986, PS guards shot and killed a retired West German army officer in FRG territory. And 2d ACR helicopters flying border patrols have been attacked by Czech jets on two recent occasions; the first attack, by a MiG-21, occurred when the Cobra strayed into Czech airspace. The second attack, by an armed L-39 trainer, took place over what was clearly West

German territory. No one was hurt in either incident.

Warsaw Pact forces also conduct airborne patrols. Usually they make border flights in utility helicopters, but both East German and Czech forces use Hind gunships on occasion. Pact border flights take off only in crystal-clear skies, and are not nearly as common as cav air patrols (call sign "Thunderhorse" for 11th ACR, "Redcatcher" for 2d ACR). Not too long ago, a couple of Czech chopper pilots defected in their Hoplite helicopter, landing in Regensburg, West Germany, asking for asylum.

The cav conducts weekly patrols with the Bundesgrenzschutz (BGS). The BGS doesn't like to be called a paramilitary force, but that's what they are — a sort of cross between the National Guard and a police SWAT team. They provide security at embassies and airports. Many tourists arriving in West Germany are startled by the sight of BGS officers toting submachine guns at the Frankfurt Flugplatz.

Bundeswehr armored cav units also screen the border, but by unwritten agreement with the Soviets they, like all regular West German military units, are forbidden to come within five kilometers of the IGB. Instead, the BGS handles the border patrols for the FRG. USAREUR cav units also work with the Zoll, West German federal customs officers. And the Bavarian Border Patrol, similar to American state highway patrol organizations, exercises civil authority along certain sections of the border and at crossings in the south.

All information from American and West German border units, military and civil, is filtered through the Border Residence Office (BRO). Each cav squadron maintains its own BRO, with input from the operations cells of the observation posts and border camps. That intelligence is consolidated at the regimental border operations center.

The Americans are interested only in military intelligence. They're there to keep an eye on the border, not the people on it. They have no civil authority. Americans on border patrol are forbidden to aid escape attempts.

Illegal border crossers — IBCs in cav parlance — would rather not have anything to do with Americans anyway, having heard horror stories about the Yankees behind the Iron Curtain. IBCs usually escape at night, wait until daylight, and then turn themselves in to West German police. If an American ground patrol runs across an IBC, he is turned over to West German authorities. In most cases the refugee is given asylum, a new identity, perhaps a job, and is relocated in the FRG.

An escape across the border is a rare event these days. The majority of escapees now are veteran East German Border Command *grenztruppen,* who know how to beat the system. Not long ago, a BC battalion commander crossed over in the 11th ACR's sector.

The Americans go by the book — in this case, the border standard operations manual (BOSOPS). With the stakes so high, there's no room for false moves or misinterpretations. On those rare occasions when border patrols from both sides come face to face across the line, they are cool, professional, neither friendly nor unfriendly. American border officers usually speak German and some Russian; Warsaw Pact officers are also generally bilingual. Nevertheless, when East meets West across the trace, they are forbidden to speak.

First Battle

To most travelers, Fulda, West Germany, is a hundred-kilometer blur off the E70 autobahn. The little city rates only a footnote in the guidebooks. There really is not much to see.

Saint Boniface, the English missionary who anointed King Pippin and brought the gospel to the Franks, is buried there. He did it the hard way. Near his tomb are all that's left of the good saint: his head, his sword, and a book of scriptures with which he tried to protect himself from his murderers. The codex is half cut through. The second thrust brought sainthood to Boniface. The futility of attempting to ward off armed force with the written word has never been so graphically illustrated. Yet, today, 1,200 years later, the last lesson of Saint Boniface must still be taught anew to each generation.

Surrounding the crypt, a cathedral and its grounds form the heart of Fulda. There are stone balustrades and towers, and huge doorways and imposing stairs that don't lead to anything anymore. They are baroque memories of little wars long gone. There will be no more little wars for Fulda.

Visitors do flock to the city, not so much for *what* it is as *where* it is. To the north is Kassel. To the south, Wurzburg. To the west, Frankfurt and the industrial Ruhr valley. To the east lies World War III.

Fulda is perhaps the only spot in the world where people come to walk a battlefield that has never seen conflict. And what they come to see doesn't exist. They're searching for nothing, the absence of something, a hole, a hollow, a . . . gap. Future historians, overachieving reporters, journalists of the cataclysmic — they've all been here, making the mandatory, preapocalyptic pilgrimage to the famous Fulda Gap.

And they are invariably disappointed. There is nothing to see. Those looking for Armageddon staring out of tank slits should head on farther east, to Berlin. Fulda is no garrison town. The 11th Armored Cavalry minds its manners, its most noisy presence confined to well outside the city center. And as for the Russians, they are not welcome here.

"Fulda's a nice town," says a Blackhorse officer. "Catholic, conservative, a real German town, full of staunch, true Germans. Russian-hating Germans. They like the Americans here."

True enough. There has been an American cav unit on the border in Fulda ever since there's been a border there. It began in 1948, when the unfortunate 14th Armored Cavalry Regiment moved in, under the old constabulary system. Things went smoothly, more or less, until the Vietnam War. All of USAREUR suffered from neglect then, but times were hardest for the 14th. Racial tension, drug abuse — the cracks that began to show in the American military monolith split wide open along the Fulda River. They sent the hard cases from Vietnam here, which is saying something.

In 1972, the Blackhorse Cav was withdrawn from Vietnam and transferred to Fulda, swapping colors with the 14th ACR, which was finally deactivated. The 11th ACR works hard to keep itself welcome. A German-American council, made up of Blackhorse commanders and sergeants major, along with the city council and community leaders, meets once a month to iron

Previous page: USAREUR is counting on high-tech equipment, such as this M2 Bradley infantry fighting vehicle, to give teeth to the new AirLand Battle doctrine.

out any problems. American soldiers are urged to make themselves at home in Fulda. Some do and some don't.

"Families are encouraged to get into the German lifestyle," says the 11th ACR adjutant. "Of course, some would rather stay closed in their little American lifestyle, but the majority of them get out and go downtown and get to know the Germans."

All the Blackhorse units have partnerships with the nearest towns, which invite the American soldiers to participate in social events. The troops

Range control tower at Grafenwohr: The Army's recent renewed emphasis on realistic training is running afoul of budget constraints.

also form partnerships with other NATO units, British and German being the most common. The idea is not to project an image as an occupational force, but rather a partner in a crusade against a larger menace. It seems to work in Fulda.

"The people here usually refer to us as 'the

1st AD DivMain, set up in a West German federal park for a CPX (command post exercise).

Fulda Regiment,' rather than the 11th ACR or whatever,'' explains a Blackhorse major. ''They consider us their unit.''

Perhaps the greatest reason the cav and the city are so chummy, however, is the presence of danger so near. It has a way of bringing people closer. There is an axiom in USAREUR that the closer you get to the border, the friendlier the Germans are. Or more supportive, at any rate, especially the older ones. The protests one sees against NATO in general, and the American military presence in particular, usually center around college campuses in the larger cities in the west and the north, well back from the line.

Most people have the wrong idea about the Fulda Gap. It is not the great turf arrow pointed at the heart of West Germany, as we have been led to believe, but rather a geographical construction, a path of least resistance from point A (East

Germany) to point B (the Rhine). The area where the East German border bulges out toward Frankfurt is actually rough country, passable only in comparison. The "gap" is, at any rate, not really near Fulda, but actually crosses the border farther north, near Bad Hersfeld.

"When Americans think of gaps, they think of things like the Cumberland Gap. That's not what this is," says a Blackhorse staff officer. "The Fulda Gap is a series of river valleys that run north and south, with very distinct hill masses."

This has historically been an invasion route because of the way the mountains run. The channelization is north and south, which is good for the defender here. But once you hit the town of Fulda, then the rivers start running east and west and it's a straight shot into Frankfurt.

The Fulda Gap winds like an anaconda, twisting to avoid rivers and *walds,* or forests. But the generally accepted path starts in East Ger-

Security is tight when the First Battle maps go up.

many, at Eisenach, where the E63 autobahn is broken up, then heads west to Bad Hersfeld, south to Fulda along the E70 autobahn and federal highway 27, and then southwest along a half-dozen decent roads into Frankfurt.

The Soviets, however, would probably not stick exclusively to paved roads. It would be too easy to halt the advance by bottling up junctions; and besides, there would be so many units coming across the border, the road network could not handle them all. Also, tanks tracks tear up pavement, and vice versa. Most likely, the main highways, if they could be secured, would be reserved for supply convoys and second-echelon forces. The armored spearhead of any Warsaw Pact invasion would come cross country.

North of Rasdorf, between Bad Hersfeld and Fulda, there is a valley about ten miles long, dominated by a half-dozen hills. The troops call it the Three Sisters. The name comes from a coarse military joke; from the air, the hills look "like three ladies lying on their backs," according to a Blackhorse scout.

But there is nothing funny about the Three Sisters. It's perfect tank country — low, rolling terrain, lightly forested but with plenty of cover. NATO possession of the Three Sisters would create a salient that would slow a Soviet assault, split their thrusts, and threaten the flanks of the advancing units. A Warsaw Pact victory would force a general withdrawal of the borderline, to prevent American units from being cut off.

Throughout USAREUR, one constantly hears talk about "winning the first battle of the next war." It's what American soldiers train for; that's why they're there, they say. The Three Sisters is that battle; USAREUR officers talk in terms of an operation "larger than Kursk" — the pivotal Eastern Front clash of armor, the biggest tank battle of World War II — or, as one armor commander puts it, a battle that would make the Israeli-Syrian struggle in the Valley of Tears "look like a command post exercise."

Just how does USAREUR plan to go about fighting the Battle of the Three Sisters? They're not saying. Not that they don't think about it — the standard U.S. command post wargame in Europe is called, interestingly enough, "First Battle." But the exercise is not open to visitors because the maps depict the units' general deployment positions (GDPs), where they would move in case hostilities broke out for real. Those positions would change according to the situation, of course; but the spacing between units, their areas of operations, and even the code names and radio call signs would give a knowledgeable observer quite a lot to go on, so guests are politely ushered out when the First Battle maps go up.

That leaves us with doctrine — how the Army says it will fight. There's plenty of that. Every ally has its own notions of how wars should be fought. The Soviets, of course, have it down to a science, or think they do. NATO doctrine, such as it is, is kept purposefully vague, not to confuse the enemy as much as themselves; serious differences in military philosophy between the NATO partners are glossed over in an effort to keep the alliance running smoothly.

Besides constant quibbles about levels of military spending and command slots, the biggest dilemma for NATO centers around two related questions: Where do we make a stand? When do we go nuclear?

These are important questions. The answers depend on where you're standing. To the French, the nuclear tripwire seems to run along their border at the Saar. The British would probably stand to see the continent overrun before risking a nuclear exchange. Living on the line gives you a particularly nihilistic attitude, however, and the West Germans might be ready to "Go Ugly Early," as they say in the F-111 boomer squadrons; after all, what's the difference between a conventional fire storm and a nuclear fire storm? When you're dead, you're dead.

Nuclear weapons have long been seen as the magic bullet for NATO planners. In the 1950s, when the West demobilized unilaterally, the overwhelming U.S. nuclear superiority was viewed as the only antidote to Soviet conventional military might. The "Fallback" strategy was just that — a general withdrawal to the west bank of the Rhine, with the east side designated a nuclear free-fire zone.

This did not sit well with the Germans, however, and when the FRG became a full-fledged military member of NATO, responsible for a

AirLand Battle looks good on paper, but will it hold up in the real world? USAREUR units, including this M1 of the 3d Mech ID, take to the field in exercises designed to find out.

15

growing share of its conventional defense, the Germans demanded, and got, a change in strategy. "Tripwire" wasn't much better than "Fallback" — it just moved the nuclear line farther up, to the center of West Germany. But a heavy dependence on nuclear weapons was cheaper than the conventional forces needed to realistically repel a Warsaw Pact invasion. With European nations unwilling to bite the bullet for nonnuclear land forces, and the United States embroiled in Vietnam, it was the best NATO could do.

By this time, France had become disgusted with NATO. Not that they had anything against nuclear weapons. In fact, the establishment of a creditable French national nuclear deterrent force led Charles de Gaulle to withdraw from the NATO military alliance in 1966. Not convinced that Americans meant what they said about risking a war that could destroy the U.S. just to save Europe, de Gaulle wanted to keep his options open. In retrospect, France's decision to keep its fingers on its own nuclear hair trigger was probably a good thing. It certainly kept the Soviets guessing, and still complicates their planning today.

With France formally out of the NATO force structure, the bulk of the alliance's conventional power now rested with the resurgent West German Bundeswehr. The Germans have been NATO's most valuable players for decades, quietly assuming an ever-growing share of the burden. They've never asked for much. But the Germans had never gotten cozy with the notion

---

Left: Results of multinational tank gunnery competitions are easy to scope out, but the NATO allies have never seen eye to eye on doctrine.

of their eastern cities held hostage to a nuclear Walpurgisnacht. So NATO strategy, which had always been *called* "Forward Defense," in deference to the Germans, now became that in earnest with "Active Defense," a doctrine of stopping any invasion as close as possible to the inner German border.

The problem with tailoring military doctrine to suit political considerations is that some facts — in this case, geography — just won't budge. Until the NATO countries learn to manipulate time and space as easily as they do the insides of the atom, anyone with a map and a calendar can see Active Defense was just Tripwire with a nuclear fuse short enough to take most of our own troops with it.

The short distance from the line to the Rhine — less than a hundred miles at its closest point near the Three Sisters — takes on frightening proportions when one considers half of it is needed for a modern mobile defense in depth. And Soviet doctrine postulates an advance of about twenty miles a day in Central Europe. To most NATO commanders, not all of them American, Forward Defense is desirable but impractical. Historically, all allied armies, and especially American armies, have needed time to organize, regroup, and generally recover from the initial shock of war before they can field effective forces.

But in West Germany there is neither the space, time, nor resources for regrouping, counterattacking, and defense in depth. By the time the needed reinforcements arrived to claim their prepositioned equipment, they'd have to fight the Russians for it. The struggle to reconcile Forward Defense with the realities of Warsaw Pact conventional warfare capabilities and new military technology has led to the greatest revi-

8th Mech ID rifleman guards a forward fuel dump. New doctrine makes such supply points high-value targets for both sides.

sion of American and NATO military doctrine since World War II.

The latest evolution of Forward Defense is called "Follow-on Force Attack" (FOFA). Although couched in typical NATO mushspeak, the concept behind FOFA is simple: Declare the old front the new rear, draw a battle line a hundred miles inside East Germany, and trade *their* cities for time. To placate politicians on both sides, the actual line is drawn closer to the inner German border than ever before.

But NATO planners don't believe there will be an actual battle line, as such. Combat will take place all along the border, a hundred miles on either side. Rear areas will be hit by air strikes and airborne raids. Reinforcements rushing to the battle will be ambushed by precision-guided munitions launched by aircraft, artillery, and stay-behind infantry teams. Units will fight isolated, cut off from supplies and communications, reeling from one battle to another.

AIRLAND BATTLE

Not coincidentally, the U.S. Army has drafted a doctrine similar to Follow-on Force Attack. AirLand Battle 2000 is the Army's latest solution to the problems of conventional land combat in a general war scenario (read Central Europe). The culmination of a U.S. Army tactical rebirth in the early 1980s, the AirLand Battle study extrapolated the Warsaw Pact threat until the end of the decade. The Army didn't exactly like what it saw. Outnumbered and outgunned, Active Defense equated with what grunts call a DIP — die in place — position.

Consider Field Manual 100-5-76, the 1976 version of the army's manual of tactical operations, written with the then-current Active Defense NATO doctrine in mind. Unimaginative, unworkable, and defensive to a fault, going by the book a decade ago meant lining up the troops like toy soldiers and waiting for the Red Wave to roll in from the east. The flanks were supposed to take care of themselves. There was no reserve to speak of, except maybe one guy back at Frankfurt with his finger on The Button. About the only good thing you could say about it was it didn't make politicians on either side angry. Military men, if they thought about it at all, thought FM-100-5-76 stunk.

After a lot more thinking and a few embarrassing exercises in which the thin green line swung like a gate before a simulated Warsaw Pact attack, the Army came up with the 1982 version of FM-100-5, the tactical embodiment of AirLand Battle

theory. The manual was an instant best-seller from the Pentagon to the trenches, a must read for up-and-coming young officers. In Europe, of course, it was a runaway hit, number one with a bullet.

The officers who drafted the latest version of the book tried hard to be as specific as possible, but, because of the subject, FM-100-5-82 was necessarily general in nature. Tantalizingly so. It has, like the story of the elephant and the blind men, a way of meaning something different to each new reader. On one point everyone agrees: AirLand Battle is wholly unlike any doctrine under which the U.S. Army has fought since the Revolutionary War.

AirLand Battle recommends fighting fire with fire, countering maneuverability with superior maneuverability, shock with greater shock. The Army looked at what it considered its strengths — the flexibility of operations afforded by superior technology and the generally higher levels of education and initiative of its officers and soldiers — and molded the doctrine around it.

Rather than trying to fix the enemy and grind it down with superior firepower, AirLand Battle recognizes that in the future there will be no front, no rear — ours or theirs. To stand still, to fight it out with wave after wave of Soviet armor attacks while the tremendous logistics needed for a war of attrition are eaten up by enemy attacks at our rear, would be a sure plan for disaster.

Instead, AirLand Battle postulates presenting a moving target, to sow confusion rather than experience it, to break up the overwhelming waves of assaults into smaller battles American forces can win.

How is this to be done? AirLand Battle empha-

Gun chief inputs artillery coordinates into the TACFIRE net. Computers are vital, if worrisome, weapons in USAREUR.

sizes four key points: initiative, agility, depth, and synchronization.

- *Initiative* is the underlying principle behind Air-Land Battle. The idea is to cause the enemy to react to your movements, not vice versa. It's a good idea, but a tough trick when you're on the defensive. The way army planners aim to get around that is to always be on the offense tactically, even if on the defense strategically. In other words, even though the tanks may be headed west, the turrets will always point east.

- *Agility* is linked to initiative in the sense that thinking faster than the other guy will give you a leg up. The notion of getting inside the enemy's "OODA Loop" is in great vogue at the Pentagon these days. The idea is to "observe, orient, decide, and take action'' faster than your opponent. It's a concept borrowed from a group of air combat experts and had a great deal to do with the design of the F-16. If you can strike while the foe is still trying to decide what you're up to, he'll always be a step behind.

Agility is a function of technology and human factors. We have the technology. The M1 and Bradleys are faster by far than anything the Soviets have. Helicopters are, of course, much faster and more unpredictable than ar-

mored columns. It's problematic determining whether communications are up to the task, but AirLand Battle sets great store by the individual unit commander, armed only with his superior's intent, fighting isolated.

• AirLand Battle's emphasis on *depth* acknowledges the fact that battles are won and lost far from what is usually considered the battle-

This M113 buzzes along at its highest speed, but only the M1/M2 combo has the necessary mobility for the Army's new emphasis on agility.

field. The new doctrine stresses depth in every dimension, not only the main battle area, but simultaneous battle in the rear — both rears. It also emphasizes depth in time, round-the-clock engagements, with no letup. The new weapons can hack the mission, technologically, with imaging infrared sights and night-vision equipment. But mechanically, it's yet to be seen if the wonderweapons are up to be driven into the ground. The same goes for the new soldiers.

- *Synchronization* means using all assets, but especially air power, not as force multipliers but as one weapon. It's harder than it looks. Inter-service rivalry is a very real threat to the U.S. armed forces. To their credit, they're giving the problem more consideration than ever before. But in a peacetime environment, squabbles over service prerogatives will always take precedent over phantom foes and imaginary battles. About all that can be done is to formulate a doctrine that *could* work, and hope the operators of the various armed forces survive the learning curve long enough to make synchronization tick, because they'll need to.

AirLand Battle doctrine combines these recently coined operational tenets with tried and true basics of warfare. Maneuver generates surprise and shock (hopefully among enemy formations and not one's own), allowing American units to seize critical positions and maintain momentum. Protection is a catchall phrase for digging in, covering up, spreading out — basic soldiercraft. Firepower is still important, but it has gone from being the army's basic reason for being to just another principle of operations, the coup de grace of a successful attack.

If what the AirLand Battle authors had in mind sounds like Napoleonics in three dimensions, you're probably right. They could have done worse. But they're going to need a lot of little Napoleons. One of the things that sets the new doctrine apart is its overwhelming emphasis on leadership at all levels.

It is hard to underestimate what a departure this is from traditional U.S. Army doctrine, a compromise between the need to field great numbers of men (and the Soviets' acceptance of rigidity to do that), and the need to field powerful armies (and the Israelis' reliance on high technology to do that). With its tremendous industrial base and almost limitless supply of citizen soldiers, the U.S. historically has taken the attitude that warfare is a trade, and can be learned as such. Destroying a bridge, for example, has been seen as not much different an operation from building a bridge: A certain amount of equipment is required, a particular set of technical and management skills is needed. Time scales and even losses can be projected. Barring some sort of secret weapon (a major American fear toward the close of World War II), the end of a world war can be projected almost to the month.

It is a philosophy that has worked well for the greatest economic power in the world. Unfortunately for the United States, their postwar rival, the Soviet Union, also sees war in much the same way — not as an industrial operation, perhaps, but certainly as a science. And, in terms of conventional warfare capability, the Russians

Right: "Band-aid" M113 stands guard against range accidents. Casualty evacuation is a nagging, unresolved question in a general war scenario.

Artillery battery commander listens to shot report. AirLand Battle stresses communication; Soviet doctrine emphasizes jamming.

are a much bigger opponent than was Nazi Germany.

With AirLand Battle, the U.S. has come to recognize that even on construction sites there are leaders. Management skills are important in war, sure, but there's still a big difference between pushing papers and leading men in battle. The concept of warrior as manager reached the heights of the ridiculous under Secretary of Defense Robert McNamara when our Army in Vietnam ditched the spirit of the bayonet in favor of something called "violence processing."

Unit pride is a lesson that has come slowly to the U.S. Army, but it's making up for lost time. It's hard to give up your life for the 128th Combat Command Team (Provisional), a unit that was formed yesterday from a pool of strang-

ers and will disband next week. But the Blackhorse Cav commands respect, especially if you're fighting alongside the same guys you went through Basic with. Shared experience will boost a unit's fighting ability more than a galaxy of Star Wars equipment. Unit cohesion starts at the smallest level and works its way up. This is what held the Germans together when everything else was falling apart. It's what holds the Brits together still.

To this end, the U.S. Army has established the COHORT program. COHORT stands for cohesion, operational readiness, and training; the idea is that the same company of soldiers goes through Basic together and, as far as possible, is rotated as a unit overseas.

The regiment, though it has no tactical role in U.S. Army hierarchy (except for units like the cav), is the repository of unit history. The Army has a new program dedicated to marrying battalions — armor, infantry, et cetera — with historical regiments. They've gone to great lengths, even creating a superregiment just for helicopter soldiers. It's hoped the regimental system will introduce élan into the soldiers' lives with a massive transfusion of tradition and ceremony. It's all part of the army's recall to glory and away from the warrior-as-manager syndrome.

There is still a lot of paper shuffling in the U.S. Army — too much, some say, but that's the peacetime army for you. And the path to

Right: Violence processor or Little Napoleon? USAREUR's return to battlefield leadership is a welcome change, but tough to implement in the absence of combat.

command is not always fast or fair. It never is. Bureaucrats always win the peacetime promotions war. But USAREUR does what it can to ferret out leaders on every level by setting up an endless round of exercises, inspections, and goals, the results of which cannot be fudged on paper. You either do the job or you don't.

What USAREUR is looking for are natural leaders — men who lead by example, officers who wait their turn at the end of the chow line, thinkers who can lay out a perfect plan like a crossword puzzle and then improvise a com-

The M557 command vehicle is for middle-level managers—in combat, company and platoon leaders ride to battle aboard their own track.

pletely different course of action from the hatch of a tank under unexpected fire. What they're looking for, in short, is the leader who implicitly understands the basic tenets of AirLand Battle as opposed to the fraud who mouths the current jargon without necessarily knowing what it means (this is called "woofing the cosmic trash," and was a popular sport among the brass in Southeast Asia).

Innovation is critical to the successful AirLand Battle commander. Although he will have some idea of what's expected of his formation, at least at the outbreak of war, who knows what's going to happen after a week or so of ambushing and being ambushed and running out of fuel, ammunition, and ideas. About the best you can say is that the enemy will have the same kinds of problems. And for a force motivated by drills, doctrine, and discipline, as is the Warsaw Pact, disintegration is a much more likely possibility.

THE AIRLAND BATTLEFIELD

AirLand Battle is a startling departure for American doctrine in that it stresses the offense above all. Defense is seen as a type of offensive operation, even though, strategically, NATO may be losing the war.

The five principal types of offensive operations are, in chronological order (and, cynics would say, in the order of their likelihood of ever being undertaken by NATO forces): movement to contact, hasty attack, deliberate attack, exploitation, and pursuit. Of these, movement to contact will be by far the most common mission for both sides. A unit is ordered to take a position somewhere or to reinforce another unit. The commander knows the enemy is likely to be in the area, but he doesn't know where, when, and how they'll meet.

As a subset of AirLand Battle doctrine, offensive operations have their own shopping list of attributes. Key is concentration — friendly forces come together only at the moment of attack, to avoid tipping their hand, and disperse immediately after to pursue fleeing enemy elements. Surprise and speed are paramount and mutually supporting; speed gives commanders the ability to hit the enemy at unusual angles, at a place and time of their own choosing. Flexibility — the ability to rapidly change direction, orientation, even going over to defense from offense — is largely a function of leadership, down to the tactical level.

The final principle of offensive operations has led to some controversy. Field Manual 100-5-82 calls audacity the "keystone" of successful offensive operations, but doesn't say much more in the way of definition. What the writers were searching for was a word to describe what they thought Soviet commanders are lacking. Perhaps audacity is not the word, but neither is taking unnecessary chances; AirLand Battle rejects tactical gambles. But if a battlefield leader feels he can seize an objective that, normally, by the book, would be beyond his grasp, *this* book gives him the leeway to try.

AirLand Battle is just part of the reconstruction of the U.S. Army, a massive restructuring of every facet of America's land forces. Collectively, the initiatives are called Army of Excellence, the greatest reforms any army has ever undertaken without the impetus of being recently soundly defeated (defeat historically being a much better molder of armies than victory).

The U.S. Army as a whole has just undergone a major reorganization based on a program called Army Studies 86. The goal was to incorporate lessons learned in recent combat and to integrate the new doctrine and equipment developed as a result. The new units produced under the reorganization are smaller, but there are more of them and, it is hoped, they will retain much of the firepower of the larger units formerly fielded.

How can this be? For one thing, the army's new weapons are clearly superior to the ones they replace. And studies have shown that, after a certain force level is achieved, many elements in a firefight become targets, not threats. Exercises with the 1st Cav at Fort Hood in the late 1970s showed that the U.S. Army's traditional five-tank platoon was not as effective as the three-tank platoon favored by the Soviets and the Brit-

ish. In the exercises only an average of two-thirds of the tanks in a five-tank platoon actually became involved in the mock firefights; all the tanks in a three-tank platoon got in shots most of the time. And the new, smaller tank platoon outscored its larger rivals, tank for tank, almost two to one.

The Division 86 tank platoon has just one

Keeping a low profile, visually and electronically, is crucial to survival on the modern battlefield. The tower supports a microwave dish connecting the HQ to its remotely sited radio antennae via data-link.

less tank than the old unit. But the new four-tank M1 platoon is more than equal to five M60s. There's an even greater reduction in the number of vehicles assigned to mechanized infantry platoons under Division 86 — two M2 Bradleys, as opposed to four APCs in platoons equipped with the older M113.

The reduction in platoon size does not necessarily mean a reduction in combat potential, merely a rearrangement. Under Division 86, the assets are redistributed, with battalions divided into four companies instead of the traditional three. Under the reorganization, the division retains the previous structure of three brigade headquarters and adds a fourth, formally recognizing the division's helicopter units as a separate brigade. The reorganization retains the division's ten maneuver battalions, but the brigade/battalion assignments are more flexible.

The reorganization not only rearranges the elements within the units, but more clearly defines the relationships between the units themselves. This is where Division 86 and AirLand Battle come together. This is where Army of Excellence will succeed or fail.

Under AirLand Battle, the corps is concerned with the biggest picture. They hold the battlefield nuclear weapons, integrate the larger surface-to-air weapons systems, allocate the corps artillery assets, coordinate major reinforcements, and interface with NATO planners. Corps commanders are three-star generals, lieutenant generals.

Corps in USAREUR are fairly typical, with maneuver elements consisting of an armored division, a mechanized infantry division, and an armored cavalry regiment. Since corps responsibilities are tied to geography as well as force, more maneuver elements could be added, but it's doubtful a corps would be constituted with less.

V U.S. Corps is headquartered in Frankfurt, as is its 3d Armored Division. The 8th Mechanized Infantry Division is headquartered at Bad Kreuznach; battalions of both heavy divisions, as well as various V Corps units, are scattered throughout the Rhine-Main valley. At Fulda, the 11th Armored Cavalry Regiment acts as the V Corps covering force.

VII U.S. Corps holds down a sizable slice of Bavaria. Its headquarters is in Stuttgart, but its real power is deployed farther east; 1st Armored Division is in Ansbach, 3d Mechanized Infantry Division is in Wurzburg, and the 2d Armored Cavalry Regiment is in Nuremberg.

The division is the heart of AirLand Battle. It is the smallest self-sustaining fighting unit; all subunits must cross-attach and depend on oth-

Technology and doctrine are important, but it all comes down to men like this.

ers for functions such as logistics and artillery support. The division is an independent command, with its own means to find, fix, and fight the enemy. It receives only the most general instructions from Corps — "invade Poland," for example — and it must come up with the plan, work out the details, and generate the orders to make it happen, or die trying.

A division is a huge, expensive, complicated bureaucracy. To move thousands of men and machines, under pressure and under fire, to execute a split-second attack acting on less than perfect information requires a team of dedicated professionals, each working on his own specialty and hoping like hell the other guy has his act together. At the division level, this team is called the general staff.

At the head of the general staff — and the division — is the commanding general (CG). A division commander is a major general, a "two-banger." He has two brigadier generals who act as assistant division commanders, usually assigned to either Maneuver (ADC-M) or Support (ADC-S). In wartime, they are more valuable as immediate replacements for the division commander, a man with an increasingly high strategic price on his head.

The divisional general staff is divided into five sections, each denoted by the prefix G: G1 (Personnel), G2 (Intelligence), G3 (Operations and Training), G4 (Logistics), and — often but not always — G5 (Civil Affairs). There are similar staffs for brigade and battalion (designated by the S prefix), but the division has additional special staff members, including the liaison officers for air defense and field artillery, and experts in engineering, chemical warfare, and signals. There are many other supporting actors who find

a home in the CG's orbit, including the chaplain, the staff judge advocate, the provost marshall, the adjutant general, the public affairs officer, the surgeon, and the finance officer.

The divisional general staff is run by the chief of staff, a full colonel. At lower levels, the battalion or brigade executive officer (XO) coordinates staff functions.

Staff duty is usually welcomed only as a means to an end. In peacetime, especially, staff officers spend much of their time bickering among themselves. There are a couple of reasons for this.

One is the simple fact that they have too much time on their hands. Take, for example, the G4. Logistics are important in peacetime, of course, and things are always needing repair or replacement. But the G4 doesn't wake up at the bachelor officers' quarters (BOQ) at Fort Riley, say, to see half his rolling stock in flames and strewn along the Missouri River, or all his carefully hoarded ordnance spent in craters along the Platte. Neither does the G2 worry about the disposition of Soviet troops in Kansas City. No, in peacetime, martial inertia sets in and staff officers, despite their intentions, usually wind up building empires out of paperwork, if only as a defense against other staff officers on a campaign to do the same.

There's another reason for staff friction. Divisional staff officers are lieutenant colonels who share the dreaded up-or-out syndrome peculiar to the American military. Whereas promotion used to be almost automatic, now the "little chicken" must compete for the limited number of high-ranking billets or take early retirement. If the lieutenant colonel can make himself useful and visible, he may be rewarded with a higher command slot of his own. If not, it's twenty years and out. Although competition is especially fierce for the primarily combat-oriented Intelligence and Operations staff officers, the G1 and G4 are also competing with others in their fields for the few bird colonel slots.

It's difficult to shine as a personnel or logistics staff officer, however, because of the bias inherent in the staff system. The ops officer is definitely first among equals on the staff, followed by the intelligence officer. The G3 tends to dominate the general staff, and a strong personality in that slot often expands his sphere of influence to everyone else's business. He may not be an empire builder by nature, but the scope of his job often means getting involved intimately with the other staff functions in order to carry it out. In fact, in the Soviet Army, the primacy of the G3 is formally recognized by naming him the deputy chief of staff.

"For the combat arms officer, this is the premier job for the division," says a USAREUR G3 officer. "I'm responsible for all the training for the division, all our operations and ceremonies — virtually all our activities."

In Europe, with the very busy training schedule that we have, we spend most of our time planning for firing, maneuvering, and training exercises — planning things that are eighteen months out and then going out and executing something we planned eighteen months ago.

AirLand Battle is very specific about a unit's responsibilities. In a major departure from previous doctrine, those responsibilities are not expressed in space but in time. For example, divisions must plan to deal within twenty-four hours with enemy forces that can affect ongoing operations in their *area of influence.* And they must be prepared to take action against forces in their *area of interest* — those that *might* affect future operations — within three days.

All this keeps the staff hopping. In the planning cycle each member of the staff deals with his specialty and makes estimates. There is often quite a bit of not-so-gentle give-and-take during these sessions, refereed by the chief of staff. The staff then presents two or three potential courses of action to the CG, along with the pros and cons of each plan. But the command decision is left to the CO.

Once a plan is implemented, it must be carried out, supervised, and more than likely changed to accommodate unforeseen developments. Divisional command and control is split among three command posts — DivTAC, DivMAIN, and DivREAR.

DivTAC is the most forward in the fight of the current battle. DivMAIN is farther to the rear and is the primary resourcing and planning HQ for the division. DivREAR is much more to the rear and is the division logistics HQ. Normally, the chief of staff is at DivMAIN, the ADC-M is at DivTAC, and the ADC-S is at DivREAR. The CG goes wherever he wants, of course.

The ultimate goal of this complex organization is to "service targets," in the current army jargon. We'll find out how they plan to do that in the next chapter.

Steel on Steel

Boy, do Russians love tanks! No kidding, they can't get enough of them. The Soviets already have more tanks than the rest of the world put together — enough to put one every ten yards across the inner German border. And they're making more every day.

Why this ardor for armor? Far be it from me to attempt to analyze the Soviet psyche in a generalist publication, but it seems there's something Freudian about this. Could it be the Russians see something of themselves in their armored monsters? Or, more specifically, how they would like to be seen: Invulnerable. Invincible. Unstoppable.

Nuts. If tanks were unbeatable, we'd all be speaking German. But there is something to be said for the notion that a country's character is reflected in its armor design. After all, tanks are built to enforce national doctrine, which itself represents what the government is willing to fight to protect.

All tanks result from engineering trade-offs among the three paramount factors of armor design: firepower, mobility, and protection. An increase in protection, for example, tends to weigh down the tank with armor, decreasing its mobility. This may be acceptable if a country's doctrine emphasizes positional defense, slugging it out toe-to-toe with advancing armor. A good example of this philosophy is Britain's new Challenger: Heavily armed. Heavily armored. And just plain heavy.

Previous page: Kicking up dust, this M1 leads a platoon out onto a firing range at Grafenwohr.

So what do the Soviet tanks tell us about Soviet thinking? To start with, they're not interested in defense — Soviet main guns can be depressed only to a very shallow angle, compared with Western tanks, making it difficult to fire from defilade or cover. On the other hand, the low turret thus made possible comes in handy on the offense by presenting a low target. The tanks can't carry too many shells, and the crew is trained only for the most basic maintenance. Soviet tanks are cramped and uncomfortable, especially in hot weather. They are relatively cheap, however, so large numbers can be fielded.

All this goes along with the Soviet "Tank as Grape" theory of armored warfare, which, stated simply, says that tanks are born to die. Soviet philosophy holds that the modern battlefield is such a dangerous place, with threats of all kinds coming from all directions, that the only real safety is safety in numbers. The Russians feel that, when it comes to technical sophistication in armored vehicles, diminishing returns set in quite quickly.

Not that current Soviet designs are primitive; the latest ones are supposed to have turbine engines and laminate armor. And there are rumors of a new Russian supertank that looks suspiciously like the one the U.S. Army has been lobbying to build. The Russians are willing to spend whatever it takes to make sure their tanks remain viable on the current battlefield, but they will not pay a ruble more.

And why should they? It could be argued that the Russians are the greatest armor experts in the world. After all, they beat the Nazis head-to-head in the largest tank battles in history. And their principal tank of World War II, the T-34, was that conflict's most successful design and

Typically awful Defense Department photo of a Soviet T-72. The Israelis got a much better look at the real thing in Lebanon and weren't too impressed with what they saw.

the progenitor of every Soviet medium tank since. Actually a prewar design, the T-34 may not have been the best; the Nazis had better tanks, but not nearly as many of them, and that's the point. The German tanks, the Tiger and the Panther, earn the admiration of hobbyists and historians. Soviet tanks command the respect of world leaders today. Which do you think is more important to the men in the Kremlin?

On the other hand, World War II was a long time ago, and perhaps modern armored warfare is passing the Soviets by. Certainly, their designs have not fared well in recent Mideast conflicts. In 1973, for example, Israeli armor on the Golan Heights destroyed more than 800 Syrian tanks in four days. For Israel, the odds were never

better than two-to-one against; in fact, on the first day of fighting, only 100 Israeli tanks stood between Israel and Syria's fleet of more than 1,000 Soviet-built tanks. Similar Israeli successes were recorded in the Sinai, after a rude reawakening to the value of combined arms operations when faced with an Egyptian force equipped with Soviet antitank guided missiles.

When the time came to build their first indigenous tank, the Israelis designed a vehicle totally different in all respects from Soviet tanks. The Merkava is huge, well armed, and built like a fortress. The turret is streamlined to present a tough target in defilade, but the hull is big enough to accommodate several infantrymen, if necessary (although the space is usually used to carry an uncommonly large load of ammunition and supplies). With its modern spaced armor and emphasis on crew safety and comfort, Merkava is built for survivability and sustained operations, quite the opposite from the relatively cheap and speedy Soviet tanks it faces on the battlefields of the Middle East.

Does this mean Merkava is a better tank in all respects? Not necessarily. Although the Israeli tank proved easily to be the best design in the invasion of Lebanon, where Merkavas of Israel's 7th Armored Brigade reportedly had no problems dispatching T-72s of Syria's 3d Armored Division, even in frontal attacks, that doesn't mean NATO gunners would have it so easy. The Russians claim that Middle East experience, though perhaps embarrassing, is irrelevant. None of their weapons systems, so the Soviets say, was correctly used by Israel's opponents, and there may be some truth in it. Russian tanks, like their planes and surface-to-air missiles, are built to fit together into a system and employed according to a highly specific doctrine. Stray from their instructions, as they claim the Syrians did, and the Soviets say they can't be responsible for what happens. But they'll sell you more tanks.

So although the Soviet tanks may not be the best tanks in the world, they are the best *Soviet* tanks in the world. And the lumbering Merkava, formidable though it may be in the biblical desert, might find it hard running the gauntlet in Central Europe. The lesson, again, is that tanks run as surely on doctrine as diesel.

That said, what do American tanks tell us about the American philosophy of tank warfare? Plenty, and not all of it good. The story starts out promisingly enough. Discounting the fleet of toy tanks produced in the 1930s, before anybody west of the Rhine knew what they were doing, U.S. armored vehicle history begins with the Sherman.

The M4 was a stalwart design — fast, roomy, easy to keep running. Its armament was light, but capable of handling just about anything it encountered on the battlefield up until 1944. Everything changed, however, toward the end of the war, when the new Nazi Panther tanks pointed out the design flaws of the Sherman in the old-fashioned way — they burned it.

Neither the Sherman's original 75mm gun nor its later long-barreled 76mm gun could come close to penetrating the German heavy tanks' armor at tactical ranges. The Nazis had no such problems. The M4's high silhouette, inadequate

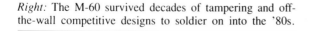
Right: The M-60 survived decades of tampering and off-the-wall competitive designs to soldier on into the '80s.

36

armor, and gasoline — not diesel — engine, made it a distressingly easy target for Nazi gunners, who nicknamed the Sherman "Zippo" because of its tendency to burn quickly.

After the war, the U.S. produced a family of tanks beginning with the M26 Pershing (which actually saw action in the closing stages of World War II), progressing through the M48 Patton to the M60, which served as America's main battle tank for more than thirty years. The tanks were not war winners, but they were contemporary, serviceable designs, which, competently crewed,

were surely the equal to anything else being fielded at the time on either side of the Iron Curtain.

Then, in the 1960s, U.S. Army tank design went completely loony. For a while it looked as if America was doomed to be the world's largest purveyor of inadequate armored combat vehicle designs. The problem was not lack of

With a fire control system and thermal sight similar to the M1, the M60A3 is a financially attractive alternative to the costly Abrams.

Allied tank crews gather annually at the Canadian Army Trophy competition to determine NATO's real Top Guns.

technological progress. On the contrary, the problem was too much progress too soon; each new design seemed to have been dreamed up by a group of mad scientists who had not seen the outside world — much less a battlefield — in years. No, what caused the U.S. to fall behind in tank design was a malady common to yuppies — purposeless ambition.

The problems started in 1963, when the U.S. Army and the Bundeswehr both decided they needed a new tank. The West Germans were the junior partners in the program, so most of the project direction — or lack of it — came from the Pentagon. And since U.S. Army doctrine at the time was rather aimless, so was the whole enterprise. Because no one knew exactly what the new main battle tank (MBT) was going to be required to do, the program became fair game for anyone with a pet weapons system to promote.

Sometimes new technology drives doctrine. Most often, doctrine dictates the kind of weapons to be built. When neither knows what it's doing, you get an armored elephant like the MBT-70.

Oh, what a tank it was! Where do we start? The MBT-70 was packed with more bells and whistles than the Batmobile. It had layered armor, a suspension that jumped up and down like an East L.A. low rider, completely stabilized fire control (the first such system, but not the first one that worked), and an autoloader that didn't work either. In the turret sat all three crew members, including the driver, who pointed the monster, when it moved, from a stabilized capsule that always faced front. And did I mention the robot AA gun?

The MBT-70 turned out to be a pretty tough tank, after all. It took eight years to kill it. And even then, the ghost of its innovative and ill-fated combination gun/missile system came back in the form of the M551 Sheridan to haunt army planners.

Light tanks have never been a wholly successful concept, mainly because they lack sufficient firepower to defeat main battle tanks. The M551 was supposed to rectify this by mounting a main gun capable of firing antitank missiles.

It was a good idea, but it didn't work. First there were problems with the missile. The MGM-51 Shillelagh packed enough punch to destroy any contemporary tank, provided it hit it, which was not often. It also suffered from an agonizingly long minimum range, up to a kilometer, while

Steel on steel: A target hulk takes hits from the Bradley's 25mm gun. Hits from Sabot rounds are less dramatic.

the gunner waited for the missile to climb back into line of sight for infrared guidance.

The Shillelagh launch tube was also used to fire 152mm conventional rounds, and that's where the problems really began. To the Army, "conventional" meant the new caseless ammunition then under development. The idea was to do away with the ports used to eject spent cartridges, thereby plugging the last remaining hole, allowing the tank to operate completely buttoned up in a contaminated environment. There was precious little room in the Sheridan to begin with, and certainly not enough to allow 152mm brass cartridges to ring around the cabin.

The caseless ammunition proved a horror story. It had a tendency to warp and jam the gun. Dud rounds were difficult to clear, especially

Left: Having grown as frustrated as the Americans with the joint MBT70 supertank program, West Germany went its own way with the excellent Leopard II.

After suffering through Sheridans and M60A2 "Starships," the Blackhorse Cav finally got *real* tanks. These M1s are on exercises near Kirtof.

in combat, where a distressing number of failures occurred (the Blackhorse Cav was the first unit to use the M551, and the damn things followed them to Fulda after they left Vietnam). Worse, the caseless shells often exploded in the breech. A quick fix only made things worse — the shells then tended to explode *in the tank,* igniting the rest of the ammunition stock. The Army's solution was to allow M551 crews to carry only one main armament round at a time — hardly an auspicious beginning.

Things got worse. In tests, the Sheridan showed inferior performance in hot weather. And in cold weather. The engine often overheated, the superchargers made a superannoying noise, crew ventilation was a problem, and the tank's electrical system was a nightmare. Even when

it worked, the gun caused problems. Crews of the M551 paid the price for the designers' attempts to flaunt the law of physics by putting such a large gun in such a small tank. With each firing, the Sheridan would literally leave the ground, coming to earth a few feet behind its firing position, thus becoming the first tank to have, and perhaps need, an "auto-retreat" feature. The dazed crew often regained their senses only to find the recoil shock had knocked out the Shillelagh's fire-control system.

The Sheridan's light armor also caused problems. Although the turret was cast from steel, the hull of the M551 was made of aluminum. The first Sheridan lost in combat was struck by a North Vietnamese mine, which ignited the highly volatile caseless ammunition inside. The ammunition could even be set off by small, anti-personnel mines. The lack of confidence the "plastic tank" engendered in Vietnam was demonstrated by the fact that, whenever they could, M551 crews rode *outside* the vehicle. Makeshift gun shields were erected around the commander's cupola, and jury-rigged armor panels were fitted to help protect the crew. Despite those efforts, on today's battlefield, with the increasing number of man-portable antitank weapons, the M551 would make an impressive pillar of smoke. If there ever was a place for a tank made of aluminum, there is not now.

The most intriguing, and tragic, part of the Sheridan saga is that, although the tank's failings were well known early in the program, the U.S. nonetheless went on to manufacture 1,700 of them. The M551 is still with us. All have been retired from active service, except for a lone armor battalion with the 82d Airborne Division (who considered America's only air-droppable tank to be so unreliable as to not be worth the trouble to drop into the relatively benign environment of Grenada). The rest of the Sheridans are in mothballs, except for a few disguised as opposing forces tanks at the U.S. Army National Training Center in California. For an American tank to end its short career in Soviet drag is a humiliating irony, but one gets the idea that army tankers, some of whom must have spent a difficult time aboard Sheridans, now secretly welcome the opportunity to shoot back at them.

The Shillelagh missile continued to decimate American armor when the army's faithful M60 was redesigned to accommodate it. The resulting M60A2 was a predictable failure, although the redesigned turret did afford better ballistic protection. Production "began" in 1966, but the troops — again, luckless European cavalry units — didn't get the first "Starships" until 1974. No matter, all 540 M60A2s are long gone now, most rebuilt almost the way they were before all the tinkering.

"Bitch'n Babe" cranks across the range at Hohenfels. The three red rubber balls on the turret mantle protect the mounts for the old night-vision equipment, no longer used.

ENTER THE ABRAMS

And so, in the 1970s, American armor was at its lowest point in history. A considerable amount of time and money had been squandered on designs that proved dead ends (an austere version of MBT-70, the XM803, was dropped after a year of development). That left only the aging M60A1, and not enough of them; many had been converted to the M60A2 standard, and many more had been handed over to Israel to make good combat losses in the Yom Kippur war.

Meanwhile, new Soviet tanks were rolling off the line every month.

Clearly, Congress was not pleased with the army's science projects. Just as clearly, something had to be done. So Congress authorized upgraded M60s as a stopgap and told the Army they could build a new tank, but they had better make it a good one this time.

Some authorities consider the M1 just another

Twilight for the gods: M60s are disappearing in USAREUR, but expect them in U.S. Army service until the end of the century.

M60 upgrade, but an M60A3 commander in VII Corps disagrees:

The M1 is a twenty-year improvement over the M60. The M60 came out in the early 60s, basically; although it's been updated a lot, it's old technology. The M1's a lot faster, at least twice as fast as an M60. The fire control's quicker, the "staid" [sight] is better. The M1's got a lot more firepower over longer ranges and it's built to go in harm's way. It's much more heavily armored, compartmentalized — it's a lot safer tank to go to war in.

Leopard I, pictured here on maneuvers, sports the same 105mm main gun as the American M60 and M1. The latest M1A1s, however, mount the Rheinmetall 120mm gun designed for the Leo II.

But the M60's a good tank. Our tanks are about five years old. They were probably originally built as M60A3s, with the improved fire-control system and the thermal sight, like the M1.

The M1 was christened "Abrams" in honor of Gen. Creighton W. Abrams, commander of

105mm Sabot rounds await loading during M1 gunnery practice. Only kinetic energy (KE) rounds can pierce the thick frontal armor of modern tanks.

the crack 37th Tank Battalion, 4th Armored Division, in World War II, Commander in Chief in Vietnam, Army Chief of Staff, and The Man Who Personally Approved the M1 Project.

A lot was riding on the M1. After the shocking loss of Israeli armor to Egyptian soldiers using cheap Soviet antitank missiles in initial stages of the 1973 war, there appeared a growing conviction on Capitol Hill and in the press that the tank was an expensive dinosaur. The U.S. Army didn't think so; had the Israelis included infantry support and evasive tactics from the first, as they did later in the war, army experts argued, they would not have been so dramatically ambushed by technology.

Besides, the U.S. Army had an ace up its sleeve. Although many civilians believed the

man-portable missile would soon shoo tanks away from the battlefield, the Army had in hand a technology that would cause just the opposite effect to take place. The name of the secret weapon: Chobham armor.

Chobham armor is so named because it was developed at the U.K.'s Military Research Center in Chobham, Surrey. Those who don't want to give the British credit for anything can call it compound armor, because that's exactly what it is — a combination of different types of armor bonded together into a shield much tougher than the sum of its parts.

Before we explain what Chobham armor is, perhaps we should explain why it works. Tanks laugh at most battlefield projectiles. Bullets, of course, bounce off. Artillery shells send fragments of shrapnel pattering across the hull like raindrops. A direct hit can do some damage, and a near miss might blow off a track or knock off some outboard equipment, such as a machine gun or an infrared (IR) searchlight. But usually an artillery barrage won't stop a determined tank attack.

If you want to kill a main battle tank, there are only two types of rounds that can do the job: kinetic energy and shaped charge. Kinetic energy is the simplest. It's a bullet. Take the heaviest mass you can find and shoot it as fast as you can at the flattest part of the tank. Chances are it'll punch through and send pieces of heavy, fast-moving metal ringing around the turret, with predictable consequences.

Mass is important in kinetic energy (KE) rounds. That's why most bullets are made of lead. Main gun rounds are a little more sophisticated. Most penetrator rods — the business end of the so-called "shoot" rounds — are milled from heavy metals, mainly tungsten carbide. The new American KE rounds use penetrators made of depleted uranium (DU), which is, as the name implies, uranium with all its harmful radioactive properties depleted (exhausted fuel core rods from nuclear power plants are a good source). Some people are still superstitious about radiation, however, so the U.S. Army has come up with the euphemism ''staballoy,'' which it prefers to use in place of ''depleted uranium.'' Whatever you call it, it's still the heaviest thing on the planet.

The penetrator rod, or dart, is about one foot long. To seal the gases in the barrel, some darts have a plate on the end, like the iron ''doughnut'' baseball players use on their bats in the on-deck circle. All KE rounds used in smoothbore guns (and some in rifled barrels) have folding fins, which spring out to stabilize the dart in flight.

The rest of the KE round consists of the charge and the sabot. Sabot is French for ''shoe''; the

Blackhorse TC (tank commander) loads up on .50-cal. before leading his crew on a qualifying drill.

"t" is silent, so it sort of rhymes with "Rambo" (the Brits call it a pot). The sabot comes in parts and fits over the penetrator rod, using its greater diameter to impart tremendous energy to the smaller dart. The larger the barrel, the bigger the charge and the more energy imparted, which is why tank guns continue to grow in size.

After the round leaves the barrel, the sabot, having transferred all its energy to the penetrator, is discarded, lest it become an aerodynamic drag. In American KE rounds, the sabot is secured by a nylon band, which melts as the round travels down the barrel. The three metal petals of the sabot are then peeled off by air resistance (which is why the front of a tank is a bad place to be for supporting infantry).

The air also ignites a tracer in the rear of the round, so tank crews can judge the fall of their shot. The penetrator flies on, hopefully to pierce the target's armor with a force no more complicated — and no less powerful — than brute physics: speed $\times$ mass = kinetic energy. (KE = $\frac{1}{2}$ MV^2)

All this is by way of explaining one of the most clangorous of all military acronyms: APFSDS-T, which stands for armor piercing, fin-stabilized, discarding sabot–tungsten. As you can imagine, this is quite a mouthful in the heat of battle, so most tank commanders, when ordering the type of round to be fired at a target, merely shout "Sabot!" and let it fly. "HEAT!" rarely heard in tank-to-tank combat these days,

---

Left: M1 gunner fires 7.62mm coaxial machine gun at Grafenwohr range.

stands for high explosive, antitank, which uses a shaped charge warhead.

In contrast to KE rounds, the shaped charge warhead is a complicated arrangement. It works on a principle called the Monroe Effect, named after the American who first came up with the idea. In order for the shaped charge warhead to work, several things have to happen in precise order. First, the round must hit the target — the more perpendicular the angle, the better. Most modern shaped charge weapons sport a long and narrow probe; the idea is for the initial detonation to shoot hot plasma through the nose, using superheat and hyperpressure to vaporize a small hole in the armor. If the tip has hit at the correct standoff distance, the rest of the charge, packed behind the probe in a copper cone, blows through the hole and wrecks the inside of the tank.

The good thing about shaped charge weapons is that they do not depend upon velocity for penetration, as do KE rounds. That's why relatively slow-moving projectiles, such as light antitank weapons and even antitank guided missiles, use shaped charge warheads. On the other hand, the round fizzles if something interrupts the shaped charge's intricate ballet of hit-penetrate-explode.

That's what Chobham armor does. "Chemical rounds such as HEAT and Saggers are completely ineffective against it," writes a former M1 platoon leader. Exactly how it works is a closely guarded secret. It's believed the armor is a laminate of several materials designed to baffle shaped charge warheads while maintaining resistance to kinetic energy rounds.

On the outside is a layer of steel, intended to set off the detonator. Most of the initial hot gas jet will vent itself in the space underneath the steel. Next comes a layer of ceramic tile, similar to that used on the space shuttle to dissipate the heat of reentry, which absorbs the superheating of the shaped charge's warhead.

This is the real secret behind Chobham armor. The principles behind compound armor have been known for decades, but the ceramic shields were too large; a kinetic energy round would shatter the ceramic sheet under the armor, caving in the side of tank and robbing it of compound armor protection. But the engineers at Chobham came up with a way around that by bonding small chips of ceramic tiles in an armored mesh, not unlike the chain mail of the armored knight. That way, only the small area impacted by the KE penetrator would be affected, and the armor would hold its integrity in all but a direct hit.

Beneath the ceramic tile is another layer of steel (or, in the improved American Chobham armor, a lightweight armor such as Kevlar) to prevent any dislodged armor from spalling the interior of the tank. This layer need not be thick; most of the warhead's energy would have been dissipated before reaching it.

The effectiveness of the shaped charge warhead is in its ability to direct a large amount of energy into a very small hole. Prevent that, as Chobham armor does, and you've got a tank impervious to just about anything on the battlefield — except another tank, armed with a powerful gun capable of accurately firing modern kinetic energy rounds, a characteristic common to less than a quarter of the heavy weapons available in a Soviet motorized rifle regiment.

There are, of course, drawbacks. Chobham armor is expensive, thick, and relatively heavy. It can be attached only to surfaces specially designed with the correct angle. For these reasons, Chobham armor is usually reserved for the front of the hull and sides of the turret.

Reactive armor, which literally blows up the shaped charge warhead before it blows up the tank, can be fitted to the sides of the hull, but it's bulky, expensive, and dangerously unpredictable, and is used only as a last resort on older tanks that cannot be fitted with Chobham. The Russians are fitting reactive armor to their older tanks, although it's not known if they've solved the problem the Israelis encountered in their initial use of reactive armor in Lebanon — premature detonation of the explosive plates by small arms and artillery fire. Simple steel fender skirts can also help defeat shaped charge rounds, provided they are set far enough away from the body of the tank so the warhead will have lost most of its energy before it hits metal again.

To move the new armor around, the M1's designers chose a turbine engine, a radical idea. Turbines have a lot going for them — they are

Bundeswehr Jagdpanzer Rakete tank destroyers have been refitted with HOT antitank missiles and renamed Jaguar 1s.

smokeless, quieter than jeep engines, quick to start, and they develop tremendous power for their size. This gives the M1 the acceleration needed to dodge antitank missiles, maneuver for flank attacks, and do a credible job of avoiding helicopters. As the U.S. Army discovered from its experience with turbine engines in helicopters, the M1s are also fairly simple machines, though not unsophisticated. And they will run on anything from jet fuel to Jim Beam.

They'll need to, because the biggest drawback to turbines is their tremendous fuel consumption. Behemoths as they are, tanks are famous for fuel inefficiency; consumption is figured in gallons to the mile rather than the other way around. The M1 is a notorious gas guzzler; while its turbine produces twice the horsepower and speed of the M60's diesel engine, it also consumes about twice as much fuel.

Because of this, and because the M1's fuel tanks are not overly large, the tank's maximum advertised cruising range on full internal fuel is estimated at about 275 miles — well below other contemporary main battle tanks (but still more than twice that of the World War II Sherman). Army experts say that's no big deal — 275 miles in one day would be a tremendous advance. Or retreat, if it comes to that.

But that's assuming M1s could refuel every day. While they may be impervious to artillery assaults, their fuel supplies aren't. Besides, mobility is highly prized in AirLand Battle doctrine.

Left: Even this gas-hogging M60 is more fuel-efficient than the turbine-powered Abrams.

How many slashing attacks can M1 platoons make with the fuel gauges stuck on E? Tanks burn up a lot of fuel sitting still, running the heaters, and charging up batteries. It is interesting to note that both the Germans and the British, no slouches in tank design, passed up turbines when it came time to choose a power plant for their new tanks.

What do you get for your gas money? Speed and lots of it. The M1 is easily the fastest main battle tank in the world. There's a story that one crew in Fort Hood, during developmental testing, outran a Texas Highway Patrol cruiser before disappearing off road. Whether or not that's true, another tank commander admits to doing sixty-five miles per hour downhill in a similarly ungoverned tank. Production M1s are equipped with a governor that limits cross-country speed to forty-five miles per hour. This not only saves engine life, it keeps the driver from barreling into situations he can't get out of.

Supertank though it may be, the M1 still rolls on treads, the soft spot of any tank. The tracks on the M1 are as protected as they can be, with special driving wheels and fender skirts (although the back skirt has been removed on all production tanks because mud accumulating on the driving wheel tended to throw the track). "Pivot steer" turns — halting one track to make a ninety degree turn — if done incautiously at high speeds can throw the track. The same thing happens when the tank tries to turn on a rock or fallen tree. The M1's special high-speed tracks are difficult to throw but just as difficult to replace, especially under combat conditions.

But the main problem with the M1's tracks is that they, unlike the rest of the tank, are vulnerable to common shaped charges. The M1's Chob-

Laying down the LAW. The M73 light antitank weapon is the grunt's personal, disposable bazooka.

ham armor may laugh at RPG rounds; the track takes them very seriously. And an M1 with a blown track is just a very expensive pillbox with a short life expectancy in combat. American infantrymen armed with light antitank weapons (LAWs) — short-range, one-shot bazookas — are taught to go for such ''mobility kills,'' and it's a sure bet Soviet foot soldiers are told the same thing.

Providing the M1 stays on track, its astonishing speed opens a whole new style of mobile, armored combat. In exercises during its introduction to USAREUR, M1s made a high-speed tour of the entire battlefield, storming from tree lines and knocking out opposing armored fighting vehicles (AFVs) before the enemy knew what hit them. A favorite tactic is hiding under cover while enemy armor passes, then using the M1's terrific cross-country speed to take them on the flanks or in the rear.

Although the M1 gets top marks for protection and mobility, some critics have questioned its firepower. Having been bushwhacked by its own weapons systems in previous attempts to replace the M60, the Army was in no mood for anything as exotic as the Shillelagh this time around. Besides, with the Chobham armor and turbine engine, the Army felt it was going out far enough on the limb of technology with the M1.

Instead, they reached for the old reliable, the M68 105mm main gun. The M68, a licensed-built derivative of the British L7 design, is the same gun used in the M60. Although the decision to go with 105mm was taken at a time when most NATO armies were upgunning to 120mm, the Army felt that, with the new Sabot ammunition, the M68 was capable of holing anything likely to be encountered on the contemporary battlefield.

Commonality *was* a concern in choosing the M68, the Army figuring that 105mm-gunned M60s, Leopard Is, and AMX-30s would vastly outnumber the new NATO 120mm-armed MBTs for a long time. When the new, big-gun Chieftains, Challengers, AMX-40s, and Leopard IIs took the field, the U.S. would be ready with a new, upgunned M1A1, armed with the same 120mm smoothbore main gun used in the Leo II. Until then the Army, which ruefully remembered its nightmare with caseless ammunition, was perfectly willing to let the Germans go through the teething process associated with the 120mm main gun rounds, which use a self-consuming case.

The Soviets are already up to a 125mm gun in their newest tanks, but a 1st AD tank com-

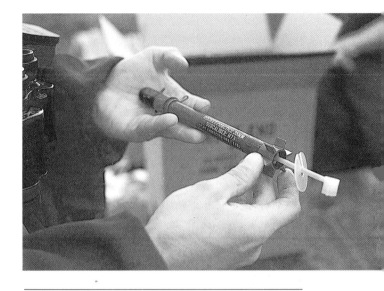

LAW practice! This subcaliber round is only slightly less effective than the real thing against the tough frontal armor of modern tanks.

mander says that's not necessarily relevant: "The Soviets believe very strongly in having the biggest gun on the battlefield. They think that's the single measure of effectiveness. But it depends how well it's designed, how good the ammunition is, and a lot of other things."

The M1 uses a gun exclusively, instead of a gun/missile system, for two very good reasons. First, the advent of Chobham armor signaled the beginning of the end for missiles with shaped charge warheads. Although no Soviet tank had been known to feature the new compound armor, the Army was not so naive as to think the West could keep it to themselves much longer.

Second, ammunition and fire-control systems had advanced to the extent that main gun rounds could perform with the accuracy and range previ-

The M1 is designed with the crew's needs in mind. Soviet tanks are built the other way around.

ously reserved for guided antitank missiles. Against tank-sized targets out to 4,000 meters, the M1 has an advertised kill rate in excess of 95 percent. On firing ranges, M1 crews are said to be able to consistently hit an eight-inch bull's-eye from well over a mile away.

Impressive though that may be, the real test of a tank is how it performs under combat conditions. Here, too, the M1 shines, scoring hits against moving targets while it is itself hurtling over the battlefield. This gives the M1 a tremen-

dous advantage over Soviet tanks, which can only fire at stationary targets while moving, and must stop to shoot at moving targets.

The M1's stabilized fire-control system is made possible by a very sophisticated main gun computer. When the tank commander (TC) spots something he wants to shoot at, he tells the crew the type of round he wants loaded and a description of the target. This sounds complicated, but usually comes out as: "SABOTTANKJEEZHURRYUP!" The loader makes sure the correct round is in the chamber and shouts "Up!" The gunner looks through his sight (which shows the same image the TC is looking at), finds the target, and reports "Identified!"

The gunner sets a switch, telling the tank what type of main gun round is selected. He presses a button on the right side of the catalacs, a sort of steering wheel he uses to aim the gun. A laser beam stabs out from the tank at the speed of light, instantly computing the range to the target.

From here on out, the M1's electronic innards take over. Provided the gunner has tracked the target for at least one second, the main gun computer automatically figures lead, range, windage, correction for temperature and barometric pressure, barrel fatigue, type of round, and gun training. The TC commands "Fire!" The gunner hits the loud button on his catalacs and shouts "On the way!" The only thing left to do after that is paint another kill ring on the barrel.

Although it sounds like it takes an eternity, the time between the TC calling the target and the gunner squeezing the trigger is only about five seconds for an average USAREUR M1 crew. Crack "gladiator" crews in NATO tournaments, such as the Canadian Cup Competition for tank gunnery, can do it even faster.

Soviet crews, however, take twice as long to get off a shot, for a number of reasons. Their tanks are harder to see out of. The automatic loader is actually slower than a human loader; plus, it has a nasty tendency to grab a gunner's private parts and try to load them into the breech instead of main gun rounds. There are a couple of steps, computed automatically in the M1, that must be performed manually by Soviet gunners. And then there's the problem of gun slew.

Turret rotation is one of those details that is not often considered by laymen but could mean literally the difference between life and death in a firefight. For all the high-tech wizardry built into today's tanks, you still have to lay the gun on the target to get a hit. In fighter aircraft today, the emphasis has changed from speed and abstract maneuverability to who can point at the adversary first; whoever gets the first shot usually wins. It's the same in tank combat. The M1's turret can swivel in a complete circle in less than four seconds. Soviet turrets are significantly slower; inside a kilometer, they can't track an M1 moving across their bow at more than thirty miles an hour.

TANK TACTICS

"We maneuver with four tanks, divided into two sections," says a tank platoon commander. "I'll take one section with my wingman and my platoon sergeant will take the other section with his wingman.

Since there are only four tanks, there aren't many what you'd call formations — there's a wedge and a line and then we split into sections and overwatch.

When contact is not expected, the platoon uses Administrative Movement — best possible speed — which is, for an M1 platoon, very fast indeed. Mostly, though, the unit travels in Tactical Formation, with its elements deployed for combat. Even when contact with the enemy is

Tank tactics in USAREUR stress teamwork. Platoons sortie in two sections, each comprised of leader and wingman.

not considered likely (never a valid assumption, according to AirLand Battle, anyway), Tactical Formation makes it easier to change over into different combat operations.

When contact *is* likely, the column splits into leading and trailing elements; one section covers the movement of the other in a technique called Traveling Overwatch. Bounding Overwatch is the same thing on a smaller scale; half the platoon takes cover and watches out for the other two tanks. In Alternate Bounds, the lead is alternately passed from element to element. In Successive Watch, one element maintains the lead, providing cover while the other catches up. The covering unit conceals itself among terrain features (the army's term for things like trees and houses),

watching out for ambushes, and relieving friendly forces pinned down by enemy fire.

When moving through known enemy territory, units may call down artillery fire on positions they can't see, just in case. Woods, towns, and the far sides of hills are typical targets for artillery prep fire. On the defense, indirect fire will be spotted on areas where the enemy might try to bypass prepared obstacles, or at bottlenecks such as bridges, roads through woods, and places where the shoulder of the highway is impassable.

On the small unit scale, warfare hasn't changed much since the time of Frederick the Great. The battle is still for pieces of ground which yesterday were insignificant but today take on monumental importance because of their location on the battle-field. Hills convey control of a large area, with good fields of fire and the ability to see the enemy before he sees you. Bridges and crossroads are the keys to movement, friendly and otherwise. Towns and woods make good strongpoints for defense and are among the few viable spots where dismounted infantry can make a stand. If nothing else, these spots must be denied to the enemy.

Tactical driving is making a comeback in USAREUR, now that doctrine allows tanks to move again. Drivers have always ranked low on the tank totem, just ahead of the loader, a mere PFC if that. Practice is important, since driving the M1 is unlike driving any other tank. Besides coping with the power and speed of the turbine, the driver sits in a semireclining position and guides the tank with a chopped-down motor-cycle handlebar.

Every division in USAREUR has at least a small range where tank crews can practice their tactical skills. But to really let loose, they load the beasts up on railway cars or heavy equipment transports (HETs) and head for Baumholder, Hohenfels, Grafenwohr, or a number of other ranges scattered across southern Germany.

Running the range can be fun, but it gets awfully familiar. The gravel has been pounded into a fine mist by generations of main battle tanks. There are brass and safety officers at every turn. Crews swear that after a couple of years in USAREUR they know every pebble on "Bowling Alley West" (Range 301 at Grafenwohr) by heart.

What they really want is fresh meat, new earth to churn. They get it about once a year, in the form of maneuver rights areas. If the ground is frozen solidly enough, if the crops are in, if NATO can persuade the local landowners, the tanks are let loose "on the economy" for an exercise.

"We go to Hohenfels to practice about twice a year. That's okay," says a 1st AD tank commander. "Sometimes there are maneuver rights areas. You can churn up a lot of dirt and cost the government a lot of money, but it's a lot of fun."

Lessons learned in the classroom come to life in the real world. Tankers begin to see how small things — like the telltale puff of smoke the M60 makes when gearing up over hills — make a big difference.

"They say use the folds of the earth, but it's kind of hard to do. You just stay low rather than high," says an M60 TC. "You don't want to stay on a prominent terrain feature like a hilltop. You'll want to go around the sides. You don't want to skyline the vehicle. There are a lot of ways you can cover areas without being up on high ground."

How does one go about displaying leadership while wallowing about inside an armored monster?

"The Soviets maneuver more in battalion-sized formations. Their commanders can be expected to be in a certain location much more often than you'd find a U.S. commander," says a 1st AD company commander. "In our doctrine, I shouldn't be up there leading the charge, so to speak. But I should be right up there, up in the hatch, unless I'm getting shot at. Then I'm down in the hatch, buttoned up, staring out the 'unity window,' trying get a picture of the horizon."

And what is he looking for?

As a tank company commander, I am most afraid of other tanks. Tanks are the most effective weapon against other tanks. Soviet antitank missiles — Saggers and so forth — generally have a very large signature. We see them and we have some time to get out of the way of their missile. We have some grenades that we can pop — vehicle on-board smoke generators — and we can return fire.

We are vulnerable to attack helicopters if they catch us by surprise in the flank. At Fort Hood we had aircraft around us all the time and it's been my experience we see them before they see us.

That's not the way the chopper pilots see it, of course. But we'll let them fight it out in the next chapter.

Boots and Saddles

Like all good armies, the U.S. Army loves to fight. If there's no war handy, they can continue their running battle with the U.S. Navy and Air Force, their traditional foes. And, failing that, they can always fight among themselves.

One of the things they're fighting over now, believe it or not, is horses. Not the flesh and blood kind; sadly, those left U.S. Army line units early in World War II (although the Bundeswehr, bless their hearts, still use pack mules to tote antitank missile launchers in mountain units). No, we're talking symbolic horses here. Images. Specifically, we're talking cavalry.

Before war became just another industrial exercise, cavalry was the star of the show. Infantry won battles and Napoleon may have had a fondness for artillery, but cavalry stirred the hearts of brave and foolish young men and contributed, tragically, to the myth of the glory of war. Hussars and lancers, dragoons and plains scouts — here was a military occupation fit for the gentleman adventurer. The thunder of hooves, the flash of sabers, those dashing uniforms; hell, if you're going to die anyway, why not go out in a blaze of glory, above the mud?

The appeal was so strong that mounted cavalry left the field decades after it ceased to perform a useful function. The fact that bravery was no substitute for armor was driven home when Polish cavalrymen broke their lances against Nazi tanks.

If the idea of cavalry is outdated, the ideal is not. The intrepid warrior is often a useful concept to governments trying to sell a war or to a service trying to buy a weapon. The cavalryman couldn't be allowed to die just because his horse was shot out from under him. So the search was on for the modern mounted hero.

The Army thought it had a winner in the fighter pilot. Here was a man, flying along on the wings of technology, into the heart of the enemy itself! The concept was so good it flew away, into the arms of the brand new Air Force. The Army kept looking.

There was always the armored cavalry. U.S. Army troopers fancy themselves the direct descendants of the plains scouts. Despite their organizational lineage, which is unquestioned, and their jargon, which often tries too hard (it's difficult to think of a million dollars worth of laminate nightmare as "Old Paint"), today's armored cavalry is nevertheless cavalry in name only. The mission has changed from charging the guns, bugles blaring, to skulking around the battlefield sneaking and peeking. Scouts they may be (although there's nothing subtle about an M1 tank), but cavalry, no.

So, what about the armor soldier? Tanks are exciting. They, more than any other weapons system, have inherited the traditional tactical roles of the cavalry — shock and exploitation. However, further examination reveals that little of the cavalryman's glory has rubbed off on the treadheads. The tank commander rumbles around with a bunch of enlisted men inside a dim metal box not much bigger than a septic tank. He may express disdain for the infantry, but he won't leave home without them, if he knows what's good for him. And today's supertanks crave so much attention, it's often unclear who is the mount and who is the rider. If the M1 were a horse, the tanker would shoot it.

Previous page: Funny, they don't *look* like horse soldiers! Tennis ball on the gunner's helmet keeps the sight cable mount from scratching the canopy.

So the search for the cavalry's successor goes on. And it is important. What the Army's really looking for is a prestige weapon, a metaphor for what it wants to be — *sleek, fast, power to burn, leading edge* — all those things civilians think the Army isn't, simply because they have had no image for it. Certainly the U.S. Air Force is no more capable at its job than is the U.S. Army. And the navy bureaucracy is still prewar in most respects. But the Air Force has fighters that are modern and classy, and is seen as such by most civilians. The Navy also has pursued prestige weapons — aircraft and their carriers, nuclear submarines, battleships — not only for the sake of prestige itself, but also to perform its worldwide commitments.

The U.S. Army had to do some serious soul-searching after Vietnam. Morale was low. Much new equipment turned out to be worthless, and old equipment was worn out. Army doctrine needed improvement at every level, from general to grunt. It was time for desperate measures. Time to call out the cavalry.

From the ashes of Vietnam, as if in answer, there rose the now-familiar muffled whopping of rotor blades snapping circles at the speed of sound. Through the shimmer of heat, the awkward Huey emerged to help lead the Army out of its funk. It was not so much the UH-1 (previously designated the HU-1, hence the name Huey) that electrified the U.S. Army, but the *idea* of the battlefield helicopter. It was new; it was high tech. It was fast, at least compared to the army's tanks and trucks. It was complicated and expensive, but legitimately so; it could do things no other machine could do. It was exciting, inspiring, and — not unimportantly — it was an *army* weapon.

Airmobile ops in Germany. The Huey was one of the Army's few bright spots in Vietnam.

The U.S. Army has done a truly commendable job in rebuilding itself. All branches have new weapons systems to keep them occupied, and, for the most part, they are creditable, often superior designs. The volunteer army works, at least in peacetime, and the officers seem motivated and professional. The new doctrine, if not as revolutionary as it sounds sometimes, is valid and recognizes the reality of war at all levels.

But there can be a case made for saying the battlefield helicopter has been the driving force behind these changes. Certainly, that's what the Army's helicopter community is saying — that the choppers inspire the troops, excite the taxpayers, set thinkers thinking, and scare the hell out of the Russians. And the Army's listening. It's buying a matched set of new helicopters and

working on more. The Army has created a whole new branch of service, the helicopter soldier, and recognized the division's air assets as a fourth brigade under the Division 86 restructuring. This means not only that chopper types will have more control over how the weapons are used tactically, but, from a more personally pragmatic standpoint, it also opens up more command slots for helicopter officers.

"[Fourth] Brigade has two attack battalions — Cobras and Scout helicopters. They're integrated with my ground maneuver battalions. Fighting

USAREUR's next generation scout chopper, the OH-58D AHIP. The mast-mounted sight is the most obvious—but by no means only—improvement.

him with tanks and aviation on different axes is one of your better schemes to defeat the Russians," says a divisional staff officer. "I don't see that this is really a great change, except that we now have a full colonel and a brigade staff that controls those two attack battalions. Before, those battalions were separate, and you'd go to them, as part of the division assets.

"It has added a new dimension to the division because we get another brigade HQ that we can use when we go out and conduct maneuvers."

An attack helicopter company commander says the change is welcome, if not yet complete: *As with any new organization, you're going to have problems with it. We're still able to execute the mission, but we need some fine tuning on the actual structure itself, the number of clerks, fuel specialists, ammo handlers. It'll work out. It's happened before and it'll happen again.*

More to the point, he says the reorganization has led to a new understanding among other army types as to how helicopters are best used on the battlefield:

By and large, the Army sees the helicopter as a flying tank. When we go out to Grafenwohr and shoot on the ranges — Range 118 or 301 — you'll see the helicopter come up, either right above the tank or right beside it, so they get a

OH-58 scout pilot straps in. The Army loves helicopters, but does it really understand them?

false impression of how attack helicopters are supposed to be used.

Very recently we had a rethinking in the division, and in USAREUR, as to how helicopters should be used in general, and attack helicopters in particular. It's starting to fall much better into the historical use of a second tier of mobility, like the old horse cavalry, or the armor in WW II, which was used as a fire brigade to put out fires, or to do a deep raid. As we're getting closer to that, I'm getting happier with the way the doctrine's changing.

HELICOPTER TACTICS

The helicopter's contribution to AirLand Battle can hardly be minimized. Speed, shock, and firepower in three dimensions are what the new doctrine is all about. Everyone agrees a strike force, consisting solely of helicopters, is a powerful new concept. Now they're working on how to put those ideas into practice. Vietnam experience is helpful, but only in a general, fog-of-war sense. Europe would be a whole new ball game.

A deep raid by helicopters is called a cross-FLOT operation, FLOT meaning forward line of own troops in army jargon. A lot goes into it. First, planners have to come up with a target that's worth risking the loss of extremely valuable men and machines. Forward arming and refueling points (FARPs) must be created near the line to make sure the short-ranged choppers have as

much fuel as possible to start with, and have a place to tank up when they're running low on the way out.

Friendly troops have to be alerted not to shoot at the force as it passes over in the dark. Night helicopter operations is an area where the U.S. Army has it all over the Soviets. Most of the Soviet air defenses depend on the operator seeing the target at some point in the loop. Darkness gives the force the edge it needs to succeed; daylight deep raids would be considered only as a last-ditch maneuver. But grunts are necessarily wary of anything flying over their heads, and since all helicopters look alike in the dark they'd have to be given a heads up not to shoot down the raiding party before it got started.

By far the trickiest part of the operation would be crossing the battle line itself, where the majority of enemy air defense weapons are positioned. A number of ruses would keep the enemy off balance. And a rolling artillery barrage would be synchronized with the operation, to keep the bad guys' heads down as the helicopters shot through. The same arrangements would have to be made, in reverse order, as the force returned to friendly territory.

"Aviation, because of its ability to get from a point to another point very rapidly, can go in pure, without any ground maneuver forces," says a USAREUR colonel. "There are some very distinct IPB [intelligence preparation of the battlefield] estimates that have to be made first to determine if he can fly over that area and have a very good chance to get in and get out, if we're going to send him in by himself.

Before you go, you're going to take a very close look at the battlefield and figure out where the enemy could be, where he would most likely

---

be, what he's going to be doing there, and is it likely that he's going to have a target there? It's a very elaborate process, but you can virtually lay it out, through a series of templates, and have a pretty good idea of what he's going to do.

Cross-FLOT operations are getting a lot of attention in USAREUR, but the most important attack helicopter mission remains antiarmor attacks in support of friendly ground forces. The typical package in USAREUR currently is a hunter-killer team of five AH-1S Cobra gunships and three OH-58 Kiowa scouts.

"There are actually seven Cobras and four scouts in the flight," says an attack helicopter company commander. "But based on maintenance and availability, we use the rule '3 + 5' in our planning and execution, because you can almost always expect two Cobras and one '58 to be down."

The helicopters work on their own, with other army ground assets, or with the U.S. Air Force, "doing JAAT." JAAT stands for joint air attack team, a mix of USAF and army aviation assets, artillery, ground air defense units, and even naval gunfire.

JAAT is the flying embodiment of AirLand Battle doctrine. Striking anywhere on the battlefield, air units can kill tanks beyond the range of ground-based defenses, or delay an enemy advance and force him to show his hand. Aviation can act as a truly mobile reserve, reacting to enemy airmobile raids or paratroop operations in the rear.

Right: OH-58 scout helicopter at speed.

JAAT doctrine is constantly changing, reflecting more the constant squabbles between air force and army planners than changing enemy threats. As it stands now, attack helicopters and air force planes will be assigned different kill zones, making it easier to conduct simultaneous attacks to saturate enemy air defenses in a communications-restricted environment. Sequential attacks may be necessary in areas of restricted visibility; they accomplish the same thing, allowing attack helicopters to reposition while the jets are keeping the bad guys busy.

Antiarmor kill zones are usually about a mile wide and about half a mile deep. Helicopters try to fire from hidden positions about two miles away, which puts them out of the range of most battlefield antiaircraft systems. Although this is getting close to maximum TOW range — 3,700 meters or so — the stopping power of the missile's shaped charge warhead is not affected by the distance. The best helicopter hides are hidden from view of enemy reinforcements and allow clear shots at the rear and flanks of tanks.

Although there are endless variations, the standard attack helicopter profile has the ships loitering behind hills and trees, rising only to squeeze off a shot. Scouts will find the targets for the attackers. If the attack helicopter can't find a target within ten seconds, it will remask, although not necessarily move to another position.

The Air Battle captain, aloft in an OH-58, is the hub of the JAAT system; he's talking to the aeroscouts in the attack helicopter teams, the air force forward air controller, the air force ground attack aircraft, and any number of ground headquarters.

"We do it in the '58, rather than the Cobra, because there's a lot more room to put a map board over here, and a frequency card over there. I've got one map book that's a foot and a half tall and eleven inches wide — you can't get that in the front seat of an AH-1," says a USAREUR battle captain. "I could fly the aircraft as well as the other pilot could, but the map, the operations order, the overlay, the graphics, the radio — that's normally the Air Battle captain's responsibility in the OH-58."

When JAAT works, it works well; artillery opens up to suppress enemy air defenses, friendly air defense artillery (ADA) watches for unfriendly fighters, attack helicopters pick off the ZSU-23 guns and other high-threat vehicles while air force jets rush in to blow up everything else. That's when it works. But JAAT doctrine is a sore point with most army aviators in USAREUR. In theory, the Air Battle captain, on the scene for hours, contacts the artillery, contacts the Air Force, and brings these elements — the attack helicopters, artillery, and Air Force — together at the same time. In theory. But . . .

"What happens is, sad to say, the bureaucracy, the interservice rivalry, is sometimes extreme," says a USAREUR scout. "In this division, it's a lot better than some other units I've seen. Normally, we can't communicate with the air force guys because the radios aren't the same. If they choose not to communicate with us, there's no way we can communicate with them."

And we've had high-ranking air force officers say air force liaison officers will control air force aircraft, period. It's a nut roll. But when it comes

AH-1F flies NOE (nap of the earth) over Bavaria. Some of the Cobra's most formidable foes wear U.S. Air Force blue.

together, it's really a very nice thing to see. Whether we can survive the learning curve long enough to make the darn thing work is a question that's certainly on everybody's mind.

There are also serious doubts whether air force A-10s can still hack the mission in Europe. The Warthog was built to take hits and can still contribute mightily in a low-threat environment. But Europe is the big leagues of air defense, and there is a growing belief that flying low and slow inside the heart of the engagement envelope of enemy air defenses in broad daylight is the key to a short, exciting life for A-10 drivers in wartime.

In the long run, the Hog will be replaced in the close air support role by the A-16, a dedicated ground attack version of the F-16 Falcon. Some A-10s will then magically become OA-10s, forward air control platforms, replacing OV-10s, which no longer have any business being near the battlefield anyway. In the meantime, Warthog drivers have finally convinced the brass that any overflight of a Soviet motor rifle division is likely to be a one-way trip, and are now receiving the weapons they have been asking for all along: long-range, fire and forget missiles like the imaging infrared Maverick.

"The new missiles have virtually turned the A-10's 30mm gun into a self-defense weapon," says a USAREUR Cobra pilot. "They can stand off at a tremendous range and lob a guided missile into the midst of an armored formation, rather than fly through a ravine and spray bullets over a very close area."

Still, the Air Force's best hopes for A-10 survivability in Europe, in the near term, rests with USAREUR and its help in saturating enemy air defenses.

"The JAAT doctrine helps the Air Force out much more than it helps the Army out," says an attack helicopter company commander. "We're willing to do JAAT with those guys, but basically our losses, as helicopter pilots, remain the same, JAAT or no JAAT. It's their losses that go down. But we still want to help them out. We want to do JAAT with them."

SCOUTS OUT

More than likely the attack helicopter team will operate on its own, given the communications problems inherent in large-scale operations. In USAREUR, that means Cobras and Kiowas: "Guns Up and Scouts Out!"

"The use of the scout aircraft is the same as scouts from the beginning of time," says an OH-58 pilot. "They find the best place for the heavies to come in, they make the liaison, they find the covered and concealed route and then it's up to the guns to move into position, get the enemy into a clear field of view, and pull the trigger."

The scout mission is not for the fainthearted. With little armor and no armament, the scouts are the first ones in and the last ones out. And with the newest laser-homing missiles, there's a good chance the attack helicopters would never come in view of the enemy. The scout, instead, "sparkles" the target with his laser, and the missile homes on the laser beams breaking up off the tank. At any rate, the scouts are exposed much longer than the attack helicopters, pointing out targets, assigning sectors, and keeping an eye out for enemy aircraft and air defenses.

There is a heated debate concerning arming the scouts. Everyone is against it except, of course, the scouts. The rest of the Army thinks hanging anything on the scout choppers will distract the pilots from their primary mission of observation. To the scouts, however, it seems silly that attack helicopters, armed and armored to the tail rotors, skulk behind hills while the fragile scouts are sent out to make sure the coast is clear. The scout helicopter is perhaps the only combat vehicle on either side that carries no weapons whatever. The grim joke among aeroscouts is that, in any future war, targets will be marked with the wreckage of a burning OH-58.

Many Vietnam-era pilots retain a soft spot for the old LOACH (light observation helicopter), the OH-6 Cayuse. Others are looking forward to the LHX, the next-generation, do-everything supercopter (sound familiar?). But what they've got is the OH-58, a helicopter no one really likes all that much. It's not that fast, not too maneuverable, and has no armor to speak of. The Kiowa was supposed to be an interim replacement for the LOACH while the Army waited for the advanced scout helicopter (ASH). The ASH never arrived; instead, its electronic gear wound up in the OH-58D AHIP (army helicopter improvement program), an airframe still not much different from the civilian Bell Jetranger.

"The only reason they call it an OH-58 is because it has the same basic airframe," says a USAREUR scout. "Everything else is changed — the rotor system, a complete new suite of electronics. They just stuck all this high-tech stuff into an old shell."

Compared with the regular OH-58, the AHIP has a more powerful engine and a tougher main rotor and tail rotor for improved maneuverability. The new main rotor has four blades instead of the original OH-58's two. The bigger tail rotor and a stability control augmentation system make the AHIP easier to control, especially in a hover, and eliminates some of the vibration for which the Kiowa is famous.

AHIP uses three methods for designating targets — forward looking infrared (FLIR), electro-optical (TV), and laser. Each crew member has a screen for the FLIR and long-range TV. As in all helicopters, the OH-58 is usually flown from the right seat. The crew member in the left seat is designated as the systems operator. The optics are contained in the mast-mounted sight, thirty-two inches above the main rotor; the systems operator slews the mast-mounted sight around with a small joystick.

The OH-58D also features a complete system for locating the aircraft, either Doppler or INS (inertial navigation system), which will prepoint the helicopter at a known target. This is invaluable, because it helps save precious seconds when the scout unmasks; it means he can get the drop on targets by seeing them before they spot him. The scout then uses the laser to designate targets for the Hellfire antitank missile or the Copperhead laser-homing artillery round, or just to point out targets to Cobras armed with TOW missiles. The laser is stabilized to help keep it aimed steadily at the designated target.

AHIP also uses burst transmission to hand off targets to attack helicopters; the typed message is electronically recorded, compressed, transmitted, unscrambled, and played back. This system comes in handy when the OH-58D is called on to serve as a field artillery aerial observer. Digital data transmission helps the AHIP receive TACFIRE messages from battalion and call the shots to the battery.

The AHIP is quite an improvement over the OH-58. Unfortunately it is expensive and scarce in USAREUR. Until its widespread arrival, scouts will have few options in the face of comm-jamming: hand signals, "cue cards," or simply pointing the nose at the enemy and hoping Cobra pilots get the message.

SNAKES

Technically, USAREUR Cobras are all AH-1S models. But there are at least four versions of the AH-1S: the modified S (with TOW missiles),

Right: Snakes coil up at a forward assembly area in southern Germany. Note the delicate TOW optics in the Cobra's nose.

the production S (with flat-plate canopy), the enhanced Cobra armament system (with 20mm gun), and the modernized S (with electronic countermeasures and infrared countermeasures equipment and air data sensor). In Germany they have all been upgraded to the latest "Step 3" standard, now referred to as the AH-1F (for fully modernized).

The Cobra started out as a nimble, lightly armed Huey conversion designed to chase Charlie around the rice paddies of Vietnam. By the time it got to Europe, the AH-1 had gained considerable weight and sophistication, its main armament, the 2.75-inch rocket, replaced by the TOW wire-guided antitank missile system, and with a three-barrel 20mm Gatling gun in place of the 7.62-inch minigun.

The Cobra still retains the 2.75-inch rocket system, but with a computerized fire-control system that offers pinpoint precision and adds some antiarmor capability to the unguided rocket.

"It's called the Hydra 70," says a Cobra pilot. "We set a time fuse, fire the rockets out to a predetermined window in space, where even though the rockets are spread out, they'll all hit the window at the same time. All the submunitions will deploy and land in a very small area.

"It's an excellent system. We can shoot it out six or eight kilometers. As long as we can put the sight on the target, we'll just tip the aircraft back and punch these rockets off. The computer has already set the fuses for us."

The Cobra has provisions for the airborne

Left: Apocalypse Wow! This gaggle of UH-60 Black Hawks looks impressive, but such a formation would be suicidal in a European war scenario.

Apache gunships will eventually replace AH-1s in USAREUR. The Cobra is a solid, but exhausted, design.

tracking laser, which slews the gunner's sight on the head-up display to the point the laser's designated — either by an OH-58D or a laser spotter on the ground. Although TOWs cannot be guided by lasers, the technology is getting to the point with the Cobra where the target can be designated and the crew can identify it, all with lasers.

The AH-1F uses the improved family of TOW missiles, slightly longer ranged with a larger warhead than first-generation TOWs. The most noticeable physical difference is the probe that extends from the warhead of TOW 2. The idea is to increase the standoff of the warhead, to increase penetration. But with Soviet improvements in reactive armor, the HEAT warhead is becoming obsolete in a frontal attack. The latest model, TOW 2+, addresses that problem by using two warheads, slightly staggered — the first one sets off the reactive armor and the second one, hopefully, penetrates the tank.

Cobras in Europe are flat olive drab (OD), with the curious shimmer of infrared absorptive paint. Markings are flat black, except for temporary unit markings that seem to be chalked in. All have the new hot metal and plume (HM+P) IR shroud, to cool and disperse engine heat and exhaust.

The AH-1F has the complete Cobra aircraft survivability equipment (ASE) defensive countermeasures suite. The ALQ-144 infrared jammer uses superheated ceramic tiles to spoof heat-seeking missiles; the slab-sided mirrorlike beacon mounted on the exhaust nozzle is called the "disco light" by the troops. The ALQ-136 is a radar jammer, using a technique called "range gate stealing" to put radar-guided missiles off the scent. And the AN/APR-39 radar warning receiver is a "military fuzzbuster" that allows Cobra crews to not only detect radar but to distinguish between types of radar and get a bearing, in degrees, of the location of the transmitter.

A new chaff and flare dispenser is being added to the AH-1F. The system is sorely needed, but it does add more weight to what is getting to be a very heavy aircraft. More than 10 percent of the Cobra's weight is devoted to armor for the aircrew — more than the weight of the weapons systems — and now pyrotechnics have been added to kick out the side windows and the crew doors in case of ditching. The new TOWs weigh more, as does the 30mm gun under consideration. All this makes for a capable platform, to be sure, but what good is an attack helicopter that can't get off the ground?

"The transmission and rotor system remain basically unchanged since Vietnam, but the aircraft has gotten heavier and heavier," says a USAREUR Cobra pilot. "There's a 10,000-pound limit on the transmission. And we're now taking off, without any armament whatsoever, at about 9,500 pounds. Obviously, as an aircraft gets heavier, the flying characteristics are worse. It's still a fast aircraft, a very maneuverable aircraft, but if you lose the engine, the autorotational techniques are lousy. You have to land the Cobra like a fixed-wing airplane or else you'll spread the skids."

There have been recent cases, in Grenada, for example, of flying Cobras at higher than mission gross weight. They had to violate the regulations to carry the armament they needed to accomplish their mission. It's getting to the point now that, unless we get a new transmission and rotor system, the Cobra will become nothing more than a very expensive taxi, because it has no payload.

A few years back, the U.S. Army recognized that the Cobra was an exhausted design and began dreaming up its replacement. The AH-64 Apache has power to burn, can hang from a rotor, see in the dark, shoot from the hip, and go like sixty. It's also nervous, terribly expensive, and has a nasty habit of throwing its riders.

"The Apache is completely different from the Cobra — different to fly, different to shoot, a completely different aircraft," says a Cobra pilot who has trained in both. "Initially, [the Army] thought they could just take older, more experienced Cobra pilots and make successful Apache pilots out of them. But they found out they had the same loss rate, same attrition rate, as if they took a brand new pilot, because the Apache system is unlike anything the Cobra ever thought about being."

The Apache is an extremely complicated aircraft. The primary weapons system is the Hellfire, a laser-guided launch and leave missile that seems to work well enough. The main gun is the chain gun, a 30mm number well suited to its role. The main fire-control system is called the target acquisition and designation sight (TADS). The night vision TADS subsystem has a 120 power thermal scope, prepointed like the OH-58D. The pilot has the pilot's night vision system (PNVS) with a monocle on his helmet, which gives him a thermal picture of the landscape, along with some symbology overlaid on the whole scene. (Cobra pilots fly with the PVS-5, a second-generation image intensifier; on a night with few clouds and a quarter moon, it works well, but a thermal system needs no ambient light at all.)

The Apache continues the Cobra convention of putting the gunner in the front seat and the pilot in the rear. But instead of putting the TADS optics on a mast-mounted sight, they built them in the chin. Why?

"Because the pilot flies the aircraft with that system," answers an attack helicopter crewman. "If you put the sight on top of the rotor system, twenty feet off the ground, the pilot has no concept of where he is in relation to the ground. The guy comes in to land this thing in the fog, and he bends the aircraft into a pretzel.

"You still have problems hovering the thing with a thermal system. People hover too high when they first start to fly an Apache, because it's sort of like having a long hood on a car."

Cobras and, eventually, Apaches, join thousands of other NATO attack helicopters to present a formidable threat to any armored assault. Plan-

ners expect each Cobra pilot to dispatch at least a dozen targets, on average, before he himself gets smoked. With attack helicopters such a valuable variable in the equation, it's no wonder NATO snakes have so many bad guys gunning for them.

THE THREATS

Number one on the hit parade is the Soviet regimental air defense systems. The latest ZSU-23-4 antiaircraft gun has a maximum range of 3,000 meters (it is no coincidence that maximum TOW range is always slightly longer than the "Zoo's" reach). The tracked guns are deployed in pairs as close as 400 meters behind leading elements of the regiment, operating in either radar-directed or electro-optical mode, using a zoom TV camera. This is especially dangerous because the first warning the pilot gets is the snap of cannon shells entering the airframe. Most likely, weather permitting, the Zoos will operate in both modes, some using radar, some firing visually.

Infrared missile systems, such as the SA-9 and SA-7, are also fired visually and give no warning. The modern SA-7 is about 4 feet long, with a maximum range of 4,800 meters and a minimum altitude of 45 meters. Cobras can probably handle SA-7s, provided they see them coming. The SA-9 Gaskin, which often works in partnership with the ZSU-23-4, takes visual ID, but has a range of 6 kilometers and a minimum

altitude of 20 meters. The SA-8 is a particularly nasty 10-foot radar missile with a maximum range of 12.5 kilometers and a minimum altitude of 50 meters.

Big missile systems found at the divisional level, such as the SA-6, are dangerous only to stupid helicopter pilots. They're looking for fixed-wing fast movers, and are unlikely to waste a valuable missile on a low percentage shot against a helicopter that needs only to descend to nap of the earth (NOE) to break lock.

Surprisingly, chopper pilots are nervous about artillery. Actually, it shouldn't be surprising; at NOE, helicopters are really just another ground target, except they are not as armored as tanks and can't dig in, like infantry. Although it's possible Soviets can intentionally target likely Cobra hides for artillery, more than likely Cobras will be hit in a barrage intended to soften up NATO defenses for a Warsaw Pact assault; attack helicopters have to get that close to shoot enemy armor with TOWs.

Soviet tankers are trained to use their turret-mounted machine gun against any target inside a mile or so and fire their main gun at anything farther away than that. Neither is likely to hit, but with enough tank crews putting up enough fire, they could get lucky. At any rate, they could make Cobra gunners nervous enough to throw the TOW off target, which is all they need. High explosive (HE) is best for this and HE shells are usually loaded in the chamber of advancing Soviet tanks. But since the automatic loader can't change ammunition, the tanks will fire whatever round is up. When the tank crew on "air alert" spots an American helicopter, everybody stops and tries to shoot it down. If they miss, the tanks crank up and jink to try to avoid the TOWs.

Left: Coordinating ground-based air defenses at Ramstein. The Sergeant York antiaircraft gun deserved to die, but that hasn't eliminated the Army's need for a modern ADA system.

Apache gunner's position. Will the AH-64 be drafted into the anti-helicopter role as well?

Massed, barrage fire is also standard practice in infantry units. It is conceivable that a whole regiment's worth of soldiers could fire at a single target. However poorly directed, that's a lot of flying steel. Couple that with Soviet advances in air defense weapons, which are getting progressively lower and more lethal, and you've got a bunch of nervous Cobra drivers on your hands. Army aviators used to assume that flying under a hundred feet would keep them safe from Soviet ADA, but no one is likely to bet his life on that now.

As if that wasn't enough, USAREUR helicopter pilots now have to look out for airborne threats. At first glance it would seem the lumbering Cobra would be just so much MiG chow against sleek jet fighters, but the lower you go, the more physics are on the side of the whirlybirds.

At low altitude, missile range is shorter and

visibility more restricted for most fixed-wing aircraft. For some, especially thick-winged ground attack aircraft such as the A-10 and the Soviet Frogfoot, turning performance is better in the thick air close to the ground. The aircraft's powerful engines, built to haul heavy loads, provide the acceleration to use the vertical plane at low altitude.

However, the high pressure of the thick air (called high q) means drag is increased, lowering the top speed of most fixed-wing aircraft, one of their main advantages over helicopters. More importantly, at ultralow levels, the use of the vertical plane for maneuver — the airplane's biggest advantage — is restricted; if they pop up too high, they might get popped by missiles or, on the way down, screw a smoking hole in the Thuringer Wald (even the ground in Europe has a Pk — probability of kill — of 100). The lesson here for fast movers is to keep your eyes open and your energy up.

So at high speed and high q, the fighter aircraft has a very small window for gun attacks on helicopters. Maximum range for a 20mm airborne cannon is typically just over two miles; at four hundred knots, the fighter pilot doesn't want to hang around the forward edge of the battle area (FEBA) anyway. They want to get in and out as soon as possible, so the fighter jock has a couple of blinks to find, track, and shoot at this unpredictable, highly maneuverable target that may or may not be shooting back. On the other hand, if the helicopter jock is asleep at the cyclic, it makes the fast mover's job a lot easier.

Missiles are another thing altogether. The whirring rotors make a perfect target for Doppler radar, as they seem to be moving in every direction at once. If the airborne radar and missile have sufficient look-down, shoot-down capability — that is, if the radar can distinguish between targets and clutter — the fast mover can just sit up in the stratosphere (over his lines) and pick off fling-wings all day. He'd just better be sure whose choppers he's splashing. In Europe, especially in the initial stages, IFF (identification friend or foe) doubts will probably preclude this type of turkey shoot.

That leaves us with infrared missiles, the weapons of choice in modern air combat. The modern Sidewinder is brilliant and tenacious, a true killer. But it works both ways. Jet aircraft are much better IR targets than modern helicopters; choppers are very well suited for the quick point-and-shoot tactics that are the only prerequisites for successful Sidewinder shots. So why not hang a couple of AIM-9s on the helicopters?

Arming helicopters for air-to-air operations is not a universally popular notion. Jealous of its prerogatives, the Air Force says bogies are its business, and helicopter fighters display a lack of confidence in USAF protection (which is justifiable). But the notion's biggest critics are in the Army itself.

ADA units say they're responsible for protecting the troops, and any effort to arm the helicopters is bound to take away emphasis and money from the needy battlefield air defense units. Some army aviators are concerned about the extra weight the missiles will add to already overburdened gunships. Others say armed scouts will be distracted from watching out for the Cobras. And everyone else in the Army, it seems, is convinced the flyboys, being flyboys, will take out after targets, in the name of self-defense, and at the expense of vital antiarmor missions.

In the end, the Army had no choice. Ironically,

it wasn't the threat of fixed-wing aircraft as much as the growing likelihood of attack by other helicopters that caused the change in army thinking. The Army now recognizes that its helicopters must be prepared to shoot down other helicopters, if only in self-defense.

HELICOPTER DOGFIGHTS

Helicopter fighter theorists are starting from a clean slate. Although air-to-air combat between

"Orange door" training Huey lays smoke during demo at Ft. Rucker. All USAREUR chopper pilots get their wings in Alabama.

gunships may have already taken place — Israeli Cobra versus Syrian Hind, for example, or Iranian Cobra versus Iraqi Gazelle — documentation is sketchy, at best. In the U.S., the marines are the acknowledged experts. Here's a sampling of what they've learned.

Aerial combat between helicopters more closely resembles catfights rather than dogfights;

they are quick and deadly, with no room for disengagement. Typically, engagements occupy less than a mile and take place, for the most part, in the horizontal plane. Reflex plays as big a role as strategy. Whoever sees and shoots first probably wins.

One-on-one engagements are possible, but multiple scenarios are far more likely, as attack teams from both sides blunder into one another over the battlefield. Considering the speeds and maneuverability of modern attack helicopters, these engagements would probably resemble the Red Baron's war, with a few important differences. With choppers flying nap of the earth, dodging behind trees and buildings, there will be an element of tank combat as well. The rapid-fire chain gun, slaved to a sight superimposed on the gunner's visor, will be useful only at extremely close range; current guns cannot be slewed quickly enough, fired fast enough, or carry enough punch to stop heavily armored gunships. Rockets, accurately aimed by computerized fire control like the Hydra 70 system, can be used against hovering targets at long ranges, but the weapon of choice will be the heat-seeking air-to-air missile.

Right now, the Army is making up for lost time by hanging the ATAS (air-to-air Stinger) on everything in sight. The missile is the same the ground troops use, without the sight. It can be aimed through the HUD (head up display) in gunships or the mast-mounted sight in OH-58Ds. At the very least it can be simply boresighted; the pilot gets an aural tone, just like a Sidewinder. When the missile growls and the pipper on the HUD blinks, the pilot lets fly.

Scouts will be armed first. They are more maneuverable and more exposed. Gunships and then utility helicopters will follow, if there are enough missiles left (or, if there's a war, enough helicopters left). The Cobras are already weighed down with TOWs and could fire them at bogies if they had to. Although TOWs are relatively slow moving and short ranged, they are not put off by ECM. And when they hit, they make a big hole in a Hind.

The AIM-9 would be the best choice. The marines use Sidewinders on their Sea Cobras for air defense. It's a better missile — faster, longer ranged, and more adept at look-down targets. But it is heavier, a bit more complex, and — this is the critical factor — an air force missile (the Chapparal is not quite the same thing). The Army already has lots of Stingers (not enough that the ADA folks are happy about giving some up, though). Anyway, given that U.S. helicopters fly NOE and Soviet choppers fly 300 feet AGL (above ground level), just about every engagement will be a look-up shot. The Stingers are certainly welcome.

The Russians are not sitting this one out either. Supposedly, they have two new attack helicopters hovering in the wings — a dedicated ground attack equivalent to the Apache and a new helicopter fighter. Believe it when you see it. Until then, the Hind is tough enough.

The Mi-24 created quite a stir when it swooped onto the scene in the 1970s. The thing is huge and heavy, unlike any gunship ever produced in the West. It can, but usually doesn't, carry a squad of troops on board, although the Hind is perfectly suited for deep strike commando raids. It's fast as hell and doesn't hover worth a damn. Maximum weight is so heavy, the Hind usually uses a rolling takeoff, like an airplane, despite its powerful engines.

Tactically, the Hind flies faster and higher than U.S. helicopters. They work in pairs or threes, attacking in a shallow dive no lower than 200 feet. Although the Hind's short wings tend to hamper performance at lower speeds, the lift from the wings at high speeds allows Hind to make turns up to three g's. The lift also enables the main rotor to snap off the boom as the airframe flexes, as has happened many times in Afghanistan.

Not that the Cobra is any better at high-g yanking and banking. The AH-1 is not a great candidate for the air-to-air role in Europe. For one thing, it is vitally needed for its primary role of antiarmor. It's already maxed out, weight-wise. And the teetering rotor severely restricts maneuverability (not to mention its danger in negative g situations — a rotor bump can kill you just as dead as a Sagger up the snot locker). Marine Cobras are twin-engined and have a little more power to spare; even so, marine Cobras are usually dedicated air-to-air fighters.

Power is not a problem with the new UH-60 Black Hawk, according to one USAREUR chopper pilot:

The Black Hawk is a tremendous improvement over the Huey. It's comparable to the Apache over the Cobra. The Black Hawk can simply lift more weight than you could ever think about loading. And it can lift a full mission gross weight with only one engine.

The story goes they got all the old Huey pilots together after the Vietnam War and said, "Okay guys, this war's winding down, let's start designing a helicopter for the next war." So the guys said, "Okay, it's got to have two engines; it's got to climb this fast on a hot, humid day, with this much load; it's got to be able to almost crashland in a landing zone, so the guy can bash it off the ground, throw the troops out and get back out again." So that's what they designed: the Black Hawk.

The UH-60 is very much Son of Huey. It is more slick, more sophisticated, and a lot more powerful. But the Black Hawk fulfills the same roles as the old UH-1, which means it does a little bit of everything, all at once — medevac missions (called dust-off), command and control, electronic countermeasures (in the EH-60 version), liaison, and supply.

It is in this last mission, hauling people and goods around the command (derisively called "ash and trash" runs in Vietnam), that the Black Hawk is most valuable to USAREUR. The latent image of the Huey in Southeast Asia has the choppers flying like locusts into hot landing zones, disgorging troops, and then whirling away. This mission, called air assault, is still viable in certain low-intensity conflicts, but in a general war in Europe it's just asking for trouble. You'll see no clouds of UH-60s over Europe. They'll come in twos and threes and, if the pilots are smart, you won't see them at all. The Hawks will make relatively short hops, mostly at night, delivering replacements and supplies — fuel bladders, rations, and above all, ammunition.

The Black Hawk can carry Hellfire missiles (but not, as yet, the laser designator) on its external stores support system (ESSS), a bolt-on wing more commonly called the ES-3. But there will be precious few Hellfires around for the Apaches when the shooting starts, so the stub wings, when fitted, usually carry extra fuel. With the extra gas, the Black Hawk can hop islands in the mid-Atlantic and deploy to Europe under its own power. It's a powerful capability, though somewhat ironic since many design parameters of the UH-60 were compromised in order to make it fit inside a C-130 for deployment.

The Black Hawk has made a smooth transition into operational use, which has given army aviation brass cause for relief. True, the UH-60 fleet has been grounded on a couple of occasions, but these appear to have been routine occurrences after accidents and are common to any aircraft. The helicopter can be dangerous in unskilled hands — *no* chopper ever has the power that pilots would like — but the Black Hawk is now firmly established as the Army's airborne armored personnel carrier (APC). Meanwhile, the Huey, which the UH-60 was to replace, is still soldiering on alongside, the latest models featuring upgrades, chiefly electronics and countermeasures, that will allow them to perform some of the more routine duties in Europe until the turn of the century.

The machines may be new, but the troops they carry have a lot in common with soldiers of Napoleon's day. Let's take a look at a breed diminishing in numbers, but not importance — the combat infantryman.

Heir to the Huey, the Black Hawk is taking over most of its roles in USAREUR. This CasEvac UH-60 is outfitted for the ''dust off'' mission.

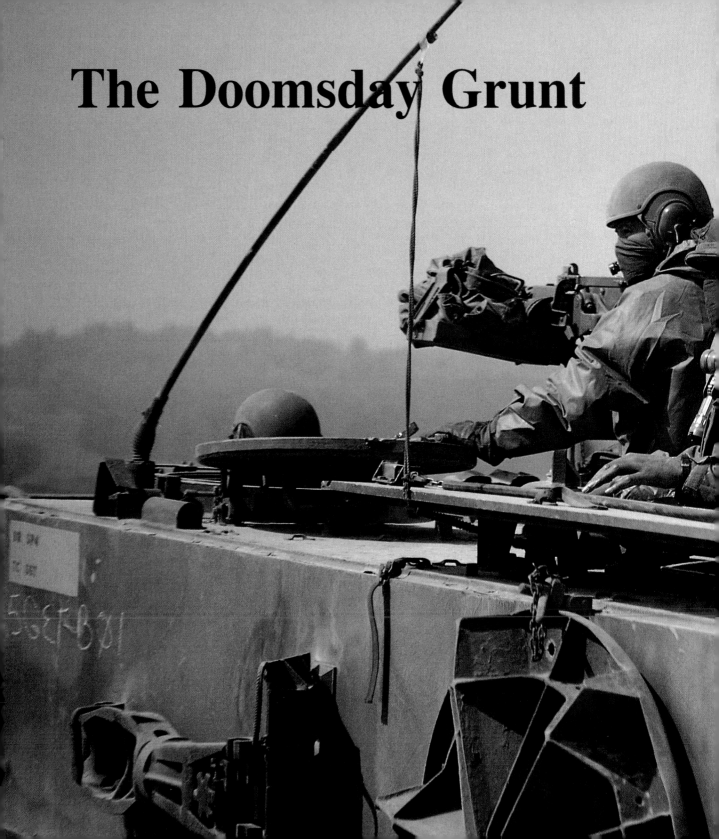

The Doomsday Grunt

Clad in his high-technology helmet, Kevlar vest, goggles, gloves, and Nomex battle dress utilities (BDU), today's Yank in Europe appears to be light years ahead of World War II's Joe and Willie. But life in the poor bloody infantry hasn't changed all that much. Despite the million dollar aluminum dragons the modern soldier rides into battle, the freeze-dried meals ready-to-eat (MREs) he wolfs down, and the immense firepower he commands, he still spends most of his combat life cold, hungry, misinformed, tired, and scared.

He is at the tip of the sword, the point of the spear, and the short end of the stick. He provokes admiration without envy. We pity him and revere him. We may question his intelligence but not his courage. He is the foot soldier, the dogface, the grunt, the infantryman.

Today's squad-level infantryman is firmly in the minority. Although in theory just about every soldier in USAREUR is also a rifleman, in practice only a small percentage are expected to face the enemy with small arms and even smaller hopes. That does not make his role any less vital. In fact, a case can be made that all the other wonderweapons and their tenders exist to support the poor doggie who actually has to walk over the ground to take it.

And take it he does. In World War II, combat infantry comprised just 10 percent of the U.S. Army, yet racked up more than two-thirds of the army's casualties. His bad luck continued through Korea and Vietnam. In World War III it could only get worse.

Previous page: The James gang rides again! Camo scarves protect this squad from the dust of the Hohenfels range.

Why does he do it? He's not stupid. Today's mechanized infantryman is the brightest recruit USAREUR has ever had. All are volunteers. Most want to make the Army their career. They may not be rocket scientists, but they can make their weapons work, which is something a lot of contractors have trouble doing.

And he's not a hero. Given the average age of today's trooper in the trenches — less than twenty years old — very few know the horror of war firsthand from Vietnam. And they've all seen Rambo. But they're smart enough to tell celluloid from cellulose nitrate, and in Europe the explosives are real. They'll fight if they have to. But they are not nearly as bloodthirsty as some officers, politicians, and editorial writers. After all, it's *their* blood.

What makes a soldier fight is quite different from what makes him join up. Today, the Army is not just an adventure. It's a job, and not a bad one. In a war, patriotism, adventurism, and not least importantly, the draft, fill the trenches. But they don't make soldiers fight.

Training makes them fight. Basic training, common to all armies, is a textbook example of psychological conditioning. Today there's more carrot than stick, but recruits are still treated like Pavlovian dogs. The actual skills learned in Basic could be taught in one afternoon to any reasonably intelligent person. What they're actually learning is conditioned response — *Locked and loaded, ready to kill. Always have and always will* — an attitude — *I want to live a life of danger. I want to be an Airborne Ranger!* What the hell, it works. He'll learn soon enough that Russians fire Kryptonite bullets.

Leadership makes them fight. In the U.S. Army, leadership comes from the ranks. Lieutenants and the occasional captain may live long enough to prove a stirring example to the troops, but it is the noncommissioned officer who kicks ass and takes names in today's Action Army. The old sarge provides a role model to the ''cherries'' — the new guys, combat virgins. The squad as a whole takes on the NCO's personality. If he's a tiger, you've got a bunch of American killers on your hands. If he's not, what you've got is a group of individual, heavily armed civil servants. A cadre of dedicated, sharp, small-unit leaders are a more formidable weapon than any baroque mechanical monster the Pentagon comes up with. And the U.S. Army is finally getting its share. The secret? They pay them enough to live on, even if there's no war going on.

More than anything, though, peer pressure makes soldiers fight. Filthy, exhausted, sick more than likely, and perpetually in shock, nothing — not love of country or fear of Sarge — is going to get the poor grunt out of his hole except for the fact that his buddies' lives depend on him. It's always been that way. Rifle squads, like man-o'-wars, are colonial animals. They are the sum of their parts. Basic training seeks to break down the individual and instill teamwork and unit pride. The grunt soon learns the only thing he can count on is his buddies, the guys he sees every day, sleeps with, eats with, fights with. Everyone else is out to get him, no matter what color uniform they wear.

In this respect, the Soviets are much worse off. Soviet troops are not led, but rather pushed. Their squad-level leadership is almost nonexistent. NCOs are basically raw recruits given slightly more training. The troops don't pay them much attention. Most Soviet NCOs don't sign up after their two-year obligation. Those who

Riflemen advance through smoke. Since biblical times, motivation has been the most important quality of successful infantry operations.

do don't earn much more respect; the troops call them ''macaroni men'' because of the service stripes on their sleeves. Officers in the Soviet Army, especially lieutenants, have to perform many of the duties that American NCOs take care of.

The Soviets rely on the dreaded political advisers to maintain morale in the trenches. Historically, political conviction ranks way down on the list of prime motivators for infantrymen in peacetime, certainly well below free food and the opportunity to make loud noises. There aren't too many fools in the Kremlin. They know how the soldiers feel about the endless drones and bleats of the *zampolit,* but it occupies time, and with such a captive audience there's always the chance some of it will sink in. As a last resort, there are always the KGB gunners in their long, black coats who follow up every advance looking for stragglers to make examples of.

The U.S. Army in Europe eschews coercion and confines itself to nagging recruits. You see it everywhere on American posts in Germany. On billboards, bulletin boards, and especially on the Armed Forces Network — radio and cable — USAREUR just won't leave the soldiers alone. *Don't drink and drive! Don't abuse your family! Watch out for credit scams!* Nag, Nag, Nag!

Don't get me wrong. These are all good ideas. And for most of the young men and women on their first hitch, West Germany is a far cry from the places where they grew up and graduated high school not too long ago. They are bright, but not too schooled in the ways of the world.

On their own for the first time, alone in a foreign land, they could easily get into trouble. Some do.

But the army's "people programs," well-intentioned fallout from the dark days of the past decade, are a bit too heavy handed. USAREUR is a lot of things, but subtle it's not. The Army can be a mother, that's true, but perhaps not in the sense it intends to be. The net effect of the dozens of peacetime preaching programs is a constant drone in the soldier's ear that eventually lulls him to sleep.

Germany is a tough tour for enlisted personnel these days. The dollar is way down. The absence

"Gladiator troops" break every rule in this VIP demo. Any airmobile operation in Europe would most likely be conducted at night, under cover, and on a very limited scale.

of any real tension has made the average German citizen indifferent, or even hostile, to the presence of the American military. GIs looking for companionship find young German women uninterested; an American boyfriend is uncool. For black soldiers, especially — and there are very many of them in USAREUR — Germany can be a lonely place, indeed.

So they retreat to the post, to its hobby shops and pizza bars and weight rooms and movie theaters, and pass the time with other soldiers. Occasionally, they will venture out to see a tiny piece of Europe, albeit an Americanized version, with a trip to one of the military resorts, like Garmisch, near the Swiss border, once the scene of the Winter Olympics.

A field exercise is actually welcomed, then, if only to break the monotony. In the field, a GI's best friend, besides his entrenching tool, is his MRE a lighter, less fatty version of the old MCI (meal, combat, individual pack). There are a dozen different "flavors" of MREs, all featuring bland, freeze-dried foods. The old C rats packed thousands of empty calories per serving. Real soldiers miss that. They *like* empty calories. So they have to eat several MREs to get that satisfied feeling.

Combat cuisine is not something Julia Child would be proud of, but you have to remember that most of these young men would probably prefer Big Macs to *cordon bleu* anyway. Those lucky dogfaces with access to hot water can make something palatable out of MREs. A favorite trick is to make a suicide stew of everything in the MRE — mashed potatoes, raisins, and chili sauce, for one execrable example — with enough hot water, salt, and pepper to disguise any intrinsic taste the mess might have.

The MRE also comes complete with matches, Chiclets, instant coffee, and a thing the troops call a "John Wayne Bar," a generic dessert the size of a gas cap that may or may not come in different flavors, despite what the package says. Some MREs are more popular than others, and there is a great rush to get to the box first to pick out the best ones. Like kids at school, the grunts swap parts of their MREs. They have evolved into a kind of currency, where vacuum-packed ham and potatoes may be worth three pork patties.

The MRE comes in a thick, brown plastic envelope designed to fit in the thigh pocket of the BDUs. Some foot soldiers grumble that the MRE is too bulky, taking up a lot of room in their rucksacks. The old C rations came in cans, which could be stuffed in socks and left to dangle from the pack frame. Mechanized infantry have it easier, stockpiling a couple of boxes of MREs — ration packs, they're called — into their Bradley or their M113.

Speaking of APCs, having a great closet on tracks clanking along behind you is a big morale booster. It eliminates a lot of short-term supply problems with assault rifle ammunition, extra antitank rounds, mines, and grenades. It's also a perfect place to stash those comforts, too big to lug around, that make life more bearable in the trenches — MREs, cartons of cigarettes and soft drinks, sleeping bags, and boom boxes.

Although the new Bradleys are light years ahead in terms of firepower, protection, and mobility, the grunts still have a soft spot in their hearts for the M113. There are just more places to put things in the old battle taxi. Space is at a premium in the Bradleys, and there's always a running battle between the mech soldiers and

The crew of "Damage Inc." takes a break from referee duties during an 8th Mech ID field exercise.

the crew for every extra square foot.

The APC is also a great source of warmth, inside and out. A favorite trick is to scoop out some soil, stick it into a C-rat can (in these days of MREs, soldiers have to use the same can over and over — another gripe), drain some fuel from the vehicle, and make a little field stove for coffee and boiling water to make the MREs edible.

The grunts could use the old steel helmets for that, but the new helmets make poor cookpots. They do, however, make great helmets, as evi-

denced by one that took an AK-47 round in Grenada without being penetrated. That helmet, now a museum piece, made the rounds and made believers of the men in the trenches.

The helmet resembles those used by Nazi soldiers in World War II, especially with the camouflage cover fitted. That's why the first grunts to

wear the helmet nicknamed it the ''Fritz.'' The name did not sit so well with the Germans, so in USAREUR it's called the ''Kevlar,'' after the brand name of the type of lightweight nylon and fiberglass laminate armor that makes it such a tough nut to crack.

The same type of armor is used in the ICM, the bulletproof vest worn by anyone who can get his hands on one. The ICM is also known by an even more obscure designation, the PASGT vest. PASGT stands for personal armor system for ground troops, and also includes the helmet and other combat accessories. The flak vest is still heavy and awkward, especially when riding around in an already cramped APC, but to the soldiers it's one of the few gestures manifested by the Army to show they are indeed interested in the lives of the poor grunts.

Although the troops wouldn't necessarily consider it as such, the rifle issued to the soldiers is actually just another ''morale weapon.'' A rifle is, in most cases, just a security blanket for a soldier; it's unlikely he'll ever get a clear shot at his opposite number. What it's good for, however, is suppressing other soldiers, keeping their heads down so they can't fire antitank weapons at the tanks he's supporting, for example. Studies have shown that the squad's real firepower comes from crew-served weapons: machine guns, antitank missiles, and the like. Left on their own, soldiers would probably never fire their weapons, or else fire them blindly in the

Meet Mr. Deuce: This soldier has taken the .50 cal. machine gun from the M113 to protect an observation post.

direction of the enemy. But two people working as a team tend to steady each other's nerves somewhat, and peer group pressure keeps their fingers on the triggers.

The M16 is one of the two most popular assault rifles in the world (the other being the Soviet AK-47) with more than five million produced. The weapon, however, hasn't proved universally popular with its users. The M16 had a nasty habit of fouling in the Vietnam jungles. That's been cleared up, but some soldiers, particularly marines, aren't happy with the M16's accuracy — or lack of it — at ranges over a quarter mile.

To remedy that, the Army has come up with a ''product-improved'' version of the M16. The

Left: Blackhorse ''gun bunnies'' hump 155mm rounds from an M992 FAASV (field artillery ammunition support vehicle). Supply duty is combat duty these days, as ''rear areas'' cease to exist.

M109 gunner checks the breech of the 155mm self-propelled howitzer.

M16A2 has a heavier barrel and shoots Belgian bullets. The new standard NATO small-arms round is the same size as the American .22 bullet (5.56mm) but has higher kinetic energy. The smaller size means soldiers can carry more ammunition in their packs and in their magazines. The Russians have gone to an even smaller caliber for their assault rifles, the AK and AKS-74, for much the same reasons.

Some critics have questioned the stopping power of the small round, but since it tumbles on impact, the little bullets can make a big hole. Man-to-man shootouts are an anomaly these days anyway, especially in the kind of war envisioned in Central Europe. Heavy weapons fire from crew-served weapons or high explosives from artillery or aircraft are the big killers. About all

that can be expected of the individual soldier is to point the loud end at the enemy and fire away. To this end, the automatic setting on the M16A1 has been replaced with a new feature that sprays three rounds in a controlled-burst pattern.

Today's soldier still lugs around a couple of other morale boosters. The new M9 bayonet is not as large as the Vietnam-era M7 it replaces, but it is twice as expensive. Worse than that, it has *no blood groove!* John Wayne must be spinning in his grave. Nevertheless, bayonet training is now mandatory for combat infantrymen, despite the fact that the doggy will probably be more likely to perform open-heart surgery with his pig-sticker than use it in close quarters. Soldiers tend to use their bayonets — and everything else, for that matter — for every purpose except the ones for which they were designed. And not just American grunts, either; the new Russian bayonet is more wire cutter than weapon, and the Israelis finally gave up and put a bottle opener on their new Uzi.

Of only slightly more use is the hand grenade. The damn thing is almost as dangerous to the man who carries it as it is to the enemy, but the grunts won't let go of it. And it does come in handy sometimes, especially in house-to-house fighting. Grenades come in several flavors, the most common being the M67 fragmentation grenade. It weighs less than a pound, with about half that being composition B explosive. There are also gas and smoke grenades, useful for signaling and concealment.

A much better idea is the new M203 grenade launcher, the replacement for the Vietnam-era M79, which fits under the barrel of the M16A2 and lobs 40mm grenades out to a quarter mile with considerable accuracy.

THE MECHANIZED BATTLEFIELD

Alone on today's battlefield, the poor grunt isn't worth much, but then neither is one multimillion dollar tank. One real-war, real-world lesson that armies around the world are desperately trying to remember in peacetime is the value of combined arms operations. Although the tank brought an end to the static tactics of trench warfare, it soon became apparent that tanks, operating on their own, were much more vulnerable than when they were supported by infantry. Foot soldiers were especially valuable in suppressing attacks on armor from other soldiers armed with cheap antitank rockets, as well as sniping at antitank gun crews to keep their heads down.

The problem with integrating armor and infantry, however, has never been solved. In World War II, mechanized infantry meant a unit had enough trucks to go around. Soldiers either rode into battle on the backs of tanks or followed closely behind them on foot. After the war, many armies developed tracked infantry carriers, better suited for cross-country operations, and enclosed them to offer some protection against artillery bursts and some small-arms fire.

But armored personnel carriers, as the postwar designs were called, were never intended to ride into battle alongside tanks. Indeed, they were seen as little more than "battlefield taxis," designed to carry infantry up to the jumping-off point, where the squad would dismount and continue the attack on foot.

The U.S. Army's M113 is perhaps the most successful Western APC. More than 60,000 were built and distributed to American allies around the world. The key to its success is that it is

Ammo rack in an M109. The piece can fire a dizzying array of projectiles, including high-explosive, antipersonnel, laser-guided and rocket-assisted shells, as well as smoke, gas, mines, and leaflets.

cheap, reliable, and, used as its designers intended, fairly effective. Troopers in Vietnam were quite fond of the idea of riding in style, toting their load in an M113 instead of on their backs, although the APC's susceptibility to mines made the troops extremely nervous at times. Israeli soldiers in the Sinai also vastly preferred the M113 to the World War II–vintage M3 half-track (which isn't saying much). They especially liked the overhead cover from artillery bombardment — so much so, they nicknamed the M113 "Zelda."

Around the 1960s, military planners began rethinking the infantry's role on the mechanized battlefield, especially under nuclear conditions. The Russians had long been fascinated with the nascent Nazi concept of mounted infantry opera-

Ample room makes the M113 APC popular in peacetime. Thin armor would make it less so in combat.

tions on the Eastern Front. Such operations would become more, not less, likely on a nuclear battlefield; to survive, soldiers would have to fight from a vehicle that could protect them from the poisoned earth and air. With both sides assuming that a conventional war in Europe would include at least tactical nuclear weapons, Khrushchev slashed the Red Army budget and ordered his generals to seriously think about the unthinkable.

What they thought up was the Bronevnaya Mashina Pehotnaya (BMP), or infantry combat vehicle. A truly original design, the BMP shocked Western military analysts when it first paraded down Red Square in 1967. Low and fast, the BMP managed to pack a squad of seven men and a turret featuring a 73mm gun and an antitank missile launcher into a package not much taller than a man. The mounted infantrymen could fire from inside the vehicle, protected from the ravages of nuclear, biological, and chemical (NBC) weapons.

The U.S. Army, bogged down in a very expensive war of attrition in Vietnam, could only look on with envy, and wonder how the Soviets did it. The truth is, they didn't. The BMP, like so many other Soviet superweapons, turned out to be a turkey. The infantrymen sat wedged between cartons of ammunition and behind magnesium doors that doubled as gas tanks, while their squad leader sat up front, cut off from his men, staring at the driver's back. The 73mm low-pressure gun was really no more accurate than a grenade launcher, and after the one ready antitank missile was fired, the gunner had to break the NBC seal to load another one (which was no big thing, because the NBC protection system, the reason for building the BMP in the first place, didn't work as advertised anyway). And, although few

---

Dug in, cammied up, and tuckered out, this soldier has the combat veteran's knack of grabbing whatever sleep he can whenever he can.

in the West were aware of it at the time, the BMP's cost — easily equal to contemporary Soviet tanks — caused a scandal in the Kremlin.

No matter. The U.S. Army immediately set about lobbying for its own infantry fighting vehicle. The trouble was, no one knew what it was supposed to look like. They didn't want to copy the BMP — for starters, most American soldiers wouldn't fit inside. Luckily, the West German Marder rolled out about this time. A big, expensive tracked vehicle armed with a 20mm cannon and, later, an antitank missile launcher on a two-man powered turret, the Marder was much closer in concept to the American infantry fighting vehicle philosophy. In fact, at one point, the U.S. Army seriously considered buying Marders. It wasn't a bad idea, but national pride and self-interest dictated the U.S. build its own.

What they came up with was the M2 Bradley fighting vehicle. It is a valuable, versatile weapons system, but it suffers from a common malady of American armor design — lack of direction. The Army, having no real experience in mounted infantry combat, didn't say, "Let's build something we can use," but rather, "Let's build something, and then we'll figure out how to use it."

What you get under those conditions is a weapon that tries to be all things to all people, even in the face of conflicting requirements. The Army wanted a vehicle small enough to transport by air but still large enough to hold a three-man crew, a seven-man infantry squad, and all their ammunition, main armament reloads, and supplies. They wanted a cheap, simple weapons system, but they insisted on including a delicate, sophisticated thermal-imaging sight, easily the most expensive feature on the M2. They gave it the firepower to stand up to tanks without giving

it the armor protection to survive should those tanks fight back.

The M2 is not viewed as a wholly successful design, especially among critics to whom MICV (mechanized infantry combat vehicle) spells "TANK." Most people see it as either a poor excuse for an MBT or history's most heavily armed airport limo. What the Bradley really represents, however, is a solution in search of a problem.

The Army should have seen it coming. The BMP proved a disaster during its combat introduction in 1973. Although the Soviets could chalk up losses along the Golan to gauche handling on the part of the Syrians (half the BMPs lost there were not hit, but simply abandoned), they had a tougher time explaining away results in the Sinai. The Egyptians went by the book there, and were rewarded with the sight of burning BMPs littered across the desert.

Soviet brass shrugged their shoulders, mumbled something that sounded like "I told you so" in Russian (they had never been crazy about the BMP anyway), and set about redesigning it into something they could use. But for American officers, it was a revelation. So the Soviets didn't know something they didn't know. The Army was on its own with the Bradley.

Current American doctrine is more than a little vague when it comes to mounted infantry combat. On the defense, it's fairly straightforward: Bradleys will drop off the troops at a good spot for them to dig in, and then go off and hide somewhere nearby (but not close enough to attract attention) to support the infantry with its gun and missiles. On the offense, the M2 will hang back on overwatch, covering the tanks with its long-range missiles and sniping at light armored

vehicles with its cannon.

Where it gets sticky is the meeting engagement, the most likely scenario in Central Europe. Do the troops dismount? When? Where do they go? What happens if their Bradley gets nailed — do they walk back? Where? How do they know when and where to remount? How do they resolve the inevitable conflict between the troops (who consider the Bradley, now empty, as their own private tank) and the crew (who consider the grunts as lunatics who have no concept of armored operations in general, and the Bradley's

The U.S. Army coveted the West German Marder before setting off on its own infantry fighting vehicle program.

vulnerabilities in particular).

The underlying problem is that, because the Bradley looks like a tank, sounds like a tank, and costs as much as a tank, just about everyone, from Capitol Hill to Objective Charlie, thinks it's a tank. It is not. The Bradley is made of aluminum. Aluminum burns. You could ground

With its TOW missile system, cosmic thermal sight, and 25mm chain gun, the Bradley can dish it out. But can it take it?

an M2 into powder and it would make excellent rocket fuel. Shaped charge weapons — rocket-propelled grenades, antitank missiles, and so on — only smudge the M1's Chobham armor. They can, however, do serious damage to an M2, a vehicle the Army said would "fight along-side" the M1. Now "alongside" has come to mean several klicks to the rear, where the Bradley will try to hide its bulk among rocks and bushes until the coast is clear. So be it. But that's not significantly advanced over what the M113 offered. And the armor is still operating without infantry support.

Forget about riding on the backs of tanks, as the GIs did in World War II. Anyone foolish enough to try that would be promptly fried by the tremendous heat put out by the M1's turbine (an infrared-guided missile, fired from Hinds, is a viable Abrams killer). The soldiers couldn't talk to the tank crew anyway — there is no telephone at the rear of the M1. It's not designed to be used that way, the Army says.

So the infantry crawls from hole to hole. It's World War I all over again. The soldier is scared of gas, helicopters, airplanes, mortars, snipers, and artillery. More than anything else, he fears artillery. Anything he can see, he figures he has a fighting chance against. But artillery rains down from the heavens. God knows where it comes from. It becomes detached, a thing of its own, separate from the war, which is merely a human endeavor. It could even come from his own guns.

Often it does. It doesn't matter. It is his constant companion in the field. It follows him from hole to hole. There is no real sleep when the ground shakes. After the war, it is the constant pounding he will remember, the incessant vibration of the earth he hardly noticed after a couple of weeks in the field. Some soldiers never forget it. And some, of course, don't live through it.

Well over half the casualties in World War II were caused by artillery. Today's pieces spit out three times the weight of fire three times as far. They shoot everything from laser-homing shells to leaflets, including mines, gas, and atomic munitions. Given the right data and enough time and ammunition, the "Redlegs" of the field artillery can neutralize anything within range, including opposing artillerymen.

Fire invites fire on the battlefield. Napoleon may have forbidden his artillery units to engage in counterbattery duels, but the invention of quick and accurate fire-locating radars have made enemy artillery batteries a lucrative target. During World War II, the Soviets favored hub-to-hub masses of towed artillery pieces, but in the last decade they've introduced two new self-propelled guns, the 122mm M1974 and the 152mm M1973, to support their mechanized forces on the move.

The U.S. Army has introduced new tactics to keep its larger batteries running and gunning on the battlefield. The platoons move and fire separately, with each platoon assigned an area one kilometer deep and two kilometers wide. The guns themselves are often spread a quarter mile apart, so that a hit on one wouldn't necessarily take out the whole battery. The battery's support vehicles — ammunition trucks and tankers — are left behind in a safer place. The guns move a great deal, often after each firing. The

---

Left: Unlimbering an M109 at Graf. The "Redlegs" of the field artillery are the infantryman's biggest nightmare.

new TACFIRE system taxes communication, logistics, and security, but it greatly increases the battery's effectiveness and survivability on the battlefield.

BATTLEFIELD ENGINEERS

If artillery is the grunt's worst enemy, combat engineers can be his best friends. Engineers can win or lose battles. Although it was once hip for military analysts to shock the press by announcing the utter uselessness of fixed defenses, today that notion is a reactionary one. Certainly strategic linear fortresses, such as Hitler's Atlantic Wall and the French Maginot line, are not worth the effort and expense it takes to build and maintain them.

But from a tactical perspective, manmade obstacles are an extremely valuable force multiplier. The Israeli's impressive Golan line stand was due in no small part to the construction of care-

fully prepared tank ditches; after the few Syrian armored bridge-layers were picked off by long-range fire, it was a simple matter for Israeli gunners to hit Syrian tanks as they wallowed in the ditch. However, Israel's overreliance on fixed defenses cost them dearly on the other Yom Kippur front. The impressive Bar Lev line across the Suez turned out to be literally made of sand. Clever Egyptian engineers used high-pressure water hoses to blast breeches in the embankment.

The idea of fixed defenses for the inner German border is undergoing a renaissance. NATO had never seriously considered the concept, mainly for political reasons; the Germans are unwilling to accept the permanent division of what many still consider one country, temporarily split by differences among foreign victors who won't go home. No one knows what lurks underground

USAREUR armored bridgelayer spans a canal during exercises. In the northern part of West Germany there is a water barrier every six miles.

on either side; but considering it is the only thing keeping apart two superpowers, each armed for Armageddon, the IGB is surprisingly free of bunkers, ditches, walls, and tank traps.

Now, however, there is a growing realization of the efficacy of fixed defenses for the trace, at least in a tactical sense. No one expects a Warsaw Pact invasion to be stopped by roadblocks, but a network of well-placed, well-designed obstacles might slow down or channel an assault. It may be politically distasteful to the West Germans and provocative to the Soviets,

Bradley crosses the Aller River over a bridge built by the 8th Engineers from Ft. Hood, Texas, during an exercise in West Germany.

but it is a cheaper way to increase security than buying more tanks, and that's why it will eventually happen.

Combat engineers are concerned with both aspects of obstacles — building them and blowing them up. The two jobs are more similar than you'd suppose. On the defense they do a lot of digging for tank defilade positions and ramps, slit trenches, tank ditches, et cetera. They use mostly civilian equipment painted green, except for the M9 armored combat earthmover, which is an armored bulldozer. On the average, one tank in each platoon will also be fitted with a dozer blade, to clear mine paths and help dig the other tanks in, because there are never enough engineers around in combat (there are not that many around, proportionally, in peacetime, and they get killed quickly). The Army also has a new engineer vehicle called SEE (small equipment excavator), a military version of the civilian Ditch-Witch.

The engineer's other main defensive weapon is the mine — antitank and antipersonnel. These come in all sizes, shapes, and types, now including chemical, with a variety of devious fuses. The idea behind mines is not to kill people and their tanks (you'd need a lot of time and mines for that) but to set them up for the kill. Older mines had to be emplaced by hand, long before the battle. New vehicles can lay mines automatically just before the engagement, for faster, more flexible operations. The Volcano system sows mines from helicopters. And new artillery-delivered mines can be spread among enemy armored formations during the fight. They don't pack as much punch as conventional mines, but they can blow tracks off tanks and even penetrate the shallow underside of some light-skinned targets.

Erecting obstacles can be dangerous sometimes. Clearing them can be suicidal. Tanks can push aside most barriers erected hastily by the troops, but it takes real engineers to break through obstacles designed by real engineers. The M728 combat engineer vehicle (CEV) is a handy beast for this type of work. It's got a winch for pulling down barriers, a dozer blade for pushing them aside, and if all else fails, a massive demolition gun for blowing the hell out of them (although not designed as a combat weapon — its fire-control system is "boresighting" or staring down the gun tube through the breech — a CEV is said to have made a "total wreck" of a North Vietnamese T-34 with its 165mm gun).

To clear mine fields, most modern armies use the "poisonous snake" approach, which is little more than a hose filled with explosives tied to a rocket. The rocket pulls the reel of hose across the mine field, where it's detonated, clearing a path. The catch is that it's expensive, short-ranged, and doesn't always work; but from an engineer's viewpoint, it's better than belly-crawling across a mine field probing with a bayonet.

Engineers are a strange breed — intelligent, resourceful, yet stupid enough to perform reverse architecture under fire. It's small wonder they are hard to come by. Both sides will probably run short of combat engineer assets quickly in the next war, even though USAREUR boasts the world's largest engineer organization, located in Frankfurt.

Engineers are especially vital in urban warfare, the nightmare of offensive-minded armies. The Soviets are so vexed they've all but given up the idea of attacking in cities altogether, in favor of bypassing them to maintain their high tempo of operations. It's probably just wishful thinking on their part. Sooner or later there's going to be city fighting in Germany, and all hell will break loose.

Or will it? Does there have to be another world war? Does there have to be another war in Germany? Does our expectation make it more or less likely? No one alive knows the answers. But we'll examine the questions more closely.

The Last War

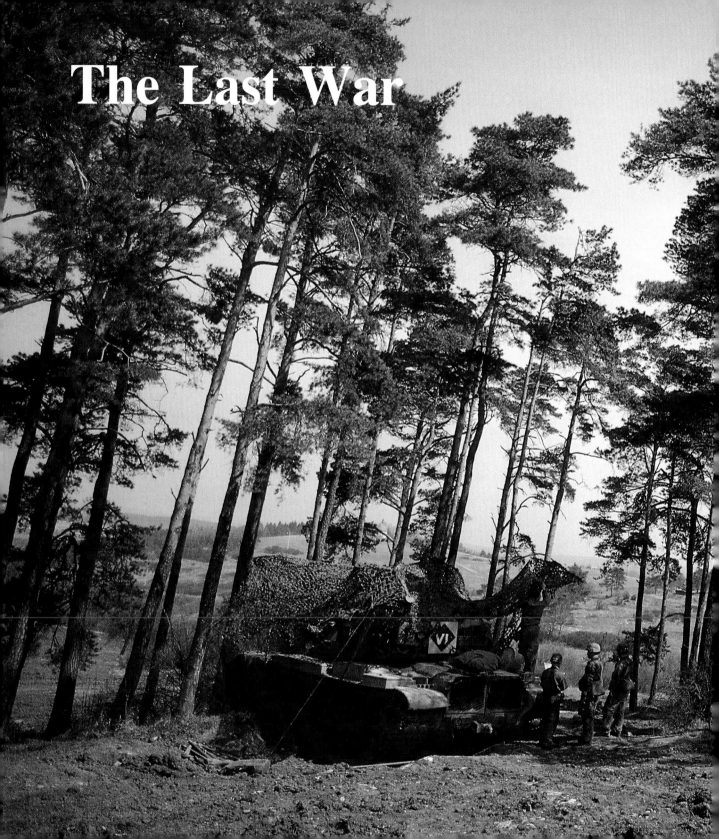

Get used to Armageddon. We fight World War III every day. Here in the Pentagon, there in the Kremlin, all through Germany — both sides — in the American desert, on the plains of Manchuria, on paper, in computers, in our heads, that war's been fought and won and lost countless times. And while we may not be getting better at preventing war, or even prosecuting it, we *are* getting pretty damn good at simulating it.

There have been wargames as long as there have been wars and games. Chess is nothing but an abstract simulation of medieval warfare. The Germans were the first to try to marry warfare to science. They quickly found there were many things about armed conflict that refused to be reduced to figures and formulae. Still, wargames can be very useful tools if used correctly. The Japanese plan of attack at Pearl Harbor was refined through gaming. They used the same system to game out the Battle of Midway. When they kept losing the game, they changed the rules. It didn't help; they lost the real battle as well.

The introduction of computers to wargaming has speeded up the process, but it hasn't made it necessarily more accurate. Garbage in, garbage out; if programmers are acting on assumptions that are not valid, neither will be the results. The Americans and the Soviets set great store by computer games and command post exercises, most of which do little but keep officers busy and out of the enlisted man's hair.

Field exercises are something else again. They

Previous page: Tank platoon of the 8th Mech ID prepares to defend typical Bavarian terrain.

are expensive and difficult to stage, but they do produce results, if only allowing the troops to go through the motions. Even something as simple as the equivalent of camping out in the unit's backyard will go a long way in demonstrating the demands the real world makes on well-laid plans. Unit cohesion is also improved; in the field, units stick together or they fall apart.

The field training exercise (FTX) is a rite of passage in USAREUR. Units are constantly going on them, getting ready for them, or regrouping after them. They are important milestones in any officer's career, from lieutenant on up. The unit is graded, officially and unofficially, on how well the men perform in the field. The pressure to look and act sharp is tremendous.

It wasn't always like that. Before, exercises were conducted with the same thoroughness and thoughtfulness as your average gym class. Units blundered about the battlefield. They paid little attention to details like scenarios, umpires, and reality. Engagements were little more than arguments over who shot whom first.

Even the opponents were lame. USAREUR troops used to fight a curious tribe of warriors called "Aggressors," who wore helmets with ventral crests, like the French constabulary, and babbled Esperanto when captured. They scooted around in strange vehicles like the "Ripsnorter" tank destroyer and the PEZO tank. The fact that the Aggressor's notional weapons bore a suspicious resemblance to real Warsaw Pact armored fighting vehicles was obvious to everyone but exercise planners. Or it could be they wanted to be polite and not offend the people whose forces they were subtly rehearsing to destroy.

No matter. After Vietnam, USAREUR decided to call a spade a spade and a Sagger a

Sagger. The Pact data charts came out of the intel lockers and back on the walls. Brigades practiced to fight a Soviet motorized rifle regiment, and they didn't care who knew it.

One of the smartest things the Army ever did was develop the multiple integrated laser engagement system (MILES). It costs a ton of money and it doesn't always work, but MILES has brought reality back to field exercises.

It works like this. A low-power laser is boresighted to the weapon — tank gun, TOW

Part of the MILES system for simulating battles, this "God Gun" allows referees to "kill" anything on the battlefield.

launcher, et cetera. It shoots a beam that is detected by receivers on the target. The beams are coded by the type of weapon, so target effectiveness and range are automatically computed. If the weapon scores a valid hit against a vehicle, its amber warning rotating light system (AWRLS) will flash.

The AWRLS is an orange safety beacon required on all tracked vehicles by federal West German law. MILES makes a virtue of this by wiring the AWRLS into the system. Not only does the tank's "whoopee light" or "party light" flash, but a valid simulated hit also disables its offensive laser. The MILES system can be reset only by referees, who sport white bands on their helmets and vehicles and carry the infamous "God Gun," the master transmitter that can kill anything on the battlefield (to simulate artillery, air strikes, and gas attacks) as well as the little green key that brings the dead back to life.

MILES has its problems. The laser (which is not exactly a laser and can't hurt anyone) can be blocked by surfaces that would not stop a real bullet. Rain can screw it up, as can any number of countermeasures dreamed up in the field by clever doggies under pressure to look good for the Old Man. But on the whole, MILES does a creditable job of simulating most engagements. It even mimics running out of ammunition by requiring the firing of a blank before transmitting a weapons firing pulse.

Unfortunately, because MILES is expensive and not easily maintained (its transmitter must be properly boresighted to the weapon it's simulating), its use is usually restricted to American firing ranges in Germany. For larger exercises, such as the NATO-wide wargames held every autumn or winter, the troops resort to the old system of umpires, combat results tables, and endless delays and arguments. To play a wargame in the field without a system like MILES is somewhat akin to playing touch football with a bunch of lawyers.

The fall wargames are a big production, usually held in conjunction with an American deployment exercise called Reforger, for REturn of FORces to GERmany (the best of all military acronyms!). Reforger is often mistaken to include the entire NATO FTX, but it is, strictly speaking, concerned only with transporting certain U.S. units earmarked to reinforce NATO in times of attack, and marrying them with prepositioned equipment. The USAREUR contribution to the wargames is called Autumn Forge; the U.S. Air Force in Europe (USAFE) equivalent is Cold Fire. The name of the games themselves changes yearly, depending upon which nation is sponsoring them.

So every autumn, after the first freeze, portions of NATO units throughout Central Europe leave garrison and tie up traffic for weeks. Near the border, especially, every highway is marked with two speed-limit signs — one for civilian vehicles (yes, they have speed limits on certain sections of the autobahn) and another for tanks and trucks in convoy. Usually a jeep flying a black and white flag starts the convoy and another one with a green flag brings up the rear. Somewhere in the endless line of plodding vehicles will be the convoy commander, distinguished by the blue flag flying on his vehicle.

Usually, the games begin with a simulated invasion that sweeps all before it, until the good guys stabilize a line and begin pushing the aggressors back. Curiously, that's exactly how the big Warsaw Pact maneuvers begin, although in those, the simulated NATO invasion is contained in the first twenty minutes or so, and the subsequent counterattack to regain ground lost takes a couple of weeks and winds up in Paris.

The NATO exercises don't seek to simulate a Pact attack exactly. The units are divided into two opposing armies, called Orange and Blue.

Orange is usually the aggressor, but no real effort is made to simulate Soviet tactics or even strategy. NATO officers are free to give it their best shot, within the limits of the scenario, no matter which side they're playing on. This has led to some interesting developments, such as the time the 11th ACR almost single-handedly conquered Central Europe, before befuddled umpires called a temporary halt to the Blackhorse rampage. It was either that or send the troops home two weeks early.

Tactically speaking, Germany is neutral ground, favoring neither attacker nor defender. There is plenty of rough country, with hills and thick woods, especially in the south, as well as large cities that, properly defended and supplied, could resist assault for a very long time. For the most part, however, USAREUR defends a tableau familiar to every wargamer — low hills and long valleys, scattered woods, and small villages.

Soldiers in MILES gear. Radioman on right wears his MILES harness backwards.

Weather is not much of a factor. It's never too hot, of course, and although Germany can be pretty frigid, it never freezes too solidly for most military operations. Bad weather plays its part mainly in reducing visibility. Throughout much of the year a thick morning ground fog covers the land like a smoke screen. Modern U.S. AFVs — Bradleys and M1s — can still move and fight, using their thermal sights. But most air operations will come to a halt in bad weather and during the night.

No matter how hard they try, no army can simulate war accurately without killing somebody. There's no substitute for the anguish, confusion, and, yes, exhilaration of real combat.

Real war is unlike Hollywood movies. The timing is all wrong. In real war they're not firing blanks, and you can actually see the rounds leave the tank guns, if you know where to look. It takes longer than you'd expect for them to hit the target. When they do, there is no huge explosion, with fire and smoke. When a sabot round hits a tank, all you see is a bright flash and a small hole in the turret. Later — much later — you hear a clang, and then, if the ammunition inside is ignited, perfect black smoke rings puffing out of the open hatch.

When artillery pieces fire, there is no lingering boom, like the processed Dolby sound in movie theaters. It's really a shock wave of compressed air you feel. It's loud enough, but it's more of a physical sensation than a sensory one. You don't hear it as much as feel it. And there's smoke everywhere. The gun chief and his gun bunnies are quickly covered with smoke and soot. The smell of cordite settles over everything.

On the other end, the explosions are something like the celluloid versions, but not nearly as dramatic. One thing they never show in movies is what happens *after* the round hits. Debris of all types, including pieces of humans unlucky enough to be caught underneath the exploding round, come pattering down from the heavens. If it was a large-caliber shell, this goes on for quite a long time.

Antitank rockets are surprisingly slow. Some sizzle off the launcher like skyrockets. Others are pushed out of the tube, slowly, and the sustainer motor kicks in downrange. They weave over the battlefield under the guidance of nervous gunners, some making wide arcs as they head for the target. It is not hard for new tanks to outmaneuver older antitank missiles. Rocket-propelled grenades and light antitank weapons are no faster, but they shoot out in a straight line. If they hit, you see a puff of smoke and an orange flash, and not much else. Later, if the target is made of aluminum or, especially, magnesium, it will burn a long time, with a bright orange flame and thick, black smoke.

Small arms are indeed small on the battlefield. The big bangs are a figment of the moviemaker's imagination. Real guns are, after all, built to make as little noise and flash as possible, and the modern ones are very small caliber — .22 for the M16. They pop. Bigger ones, like "Mr. Deuce," the .50-caliber M2 HB, or the comparable Soviet "Dushka," still make a sizable chatter. You can see the tracers from some of these, but it's a double-edged sword — tracers make aiming easier, but they also betray the firer's position.

Antiaircraft weapons have their own signature. Fighter pilots in Vietnam could tell what was shooting at them by the appearance of the exploding rounds: 23mm came up in clips of five, with bright orange balls; 37mm showed up as bright white sparkles, with no smoke. Big black puffs with red inside meant larger caliber triple-A.

A Hawk launching is loud and bright. It gets airborne in a hurry and then comes down on its prey with no telltale smoke. The SA-7s poke around the sky; they can be outrun. Stingers have no smoke and little flame; they are extremely difficult to spot.

Attack helicopters, especially the new Apaches, are surprisingly quiet. At maximum TOW range they almost never will have been spotted before they get off a shot. Two miles away and head-on, a Cobra is almost impossible to pick out, even if you know where to look. It works both ways; gunners must use their telescopic sights to pick out most targets, and with the danger and vibration inherent in a pop-up maneuver, many targets go unnoticed.

In all, Hollywood does the real world a disservice by depicting modern battles at Civil War ranges. Chances are most soldiers will never see whom they're shooting at, will never know if they hit him or not. And most grunts won't know what hit them. On the small scale, battle is chaotic. Winning or losing is too broad a concept below the platoon level. Soldiers won't know who's winning the current battle. Neither will they be told. Neither will they care. They will be ordered from place to place, to different degrees of relative danger and safety, until they are killed, captured (unlikely, next time), or relieved. Such is the life of a soldier on either side.

Officers won't know much more. AirLand Battle pretty much admits things will get out of hand rapidly. Reconnaissance elements will be quickly expended. News reports will be totally

This M1 from the 3d AD lets one fly on Range 301 at Grafenwohr.

inaccurate. The roads will be clogged in both directions with refugees, alive or otherwise. The airwaves will be saturated with calls for more ammunition, fuel, supplies, and medical aid. After two weeks, the war will wind down to short spasms of violence scattered along the line. The few supply shipments that are not at the bottom of the North Atlantic or burning by the twisted rails of the Volga line will be consumed immediately by those few units still in action.

The truth is, war is pointless, but war in Europe even more so. There's plenty worth fighting about and nothing fighting will settle. If there was ever such a thing as a stabilized front, Central Europe is it. A century of hard fighting and hard feelings has forged a solid understanding among the antagonists. They've learned from their mistakes.

World War I took place automatically, irresistibly, a function of alliances and mobilization schedules that, once undertaken, could not be reversed. It was very much like the programmed trading that caused the huge losses on Wall Street on Black Monday. Now we have crisis management and hot lines and mechanisms that pretty much assure, in Europe at least, that no one will go to war without meaning to.

World War II was a religious war. The Nazis were godless, true, but the feelings they evoked among their followers and opponents were fanati-

Vulcan ADA gunner stands watch at USAFE airfield. A real world mission keeps USAREUR sharp.

cal. It was easy to take sides, and there were plenty of people willing to die, or kill, for their beliefs. There are no more fanatics now. The West is firmly secular. The Eastern bloc is half-heartedly into socialism as a cryptoreligion; but outside of a few zealots in the Kremlin, no one is ready to die for the Communist dialectic.

So what's the fuss about? War in Europe is

one of the world's bad habits. People are always fighting about something there. Chances are if there is a World War III, it will come out of nowhere over something no one can imagine yet. Presently, there are only a few scenarios that would guarantee a general war in Europe. They are acknowledged by both sides, and great pains are taken to make sure the situation is stabilized.

The central question, still unresolved, is what to do about Berlin. USAREUR has a brigade there. The French and British also maintain a military presence, deep in the heart of Iron Curtain country. It is an artificial situation — the kind of vacuum that human nature abhors. The Russians see Berlin as theirs, by dint of geography, if nothing else. The allies don't agree. Fifty years of living together have resulted in a workable, if fragile, peace. Although neither side is happy with the status quo, they are satisfied and would no doubt resist, by force of arms if necessary, any unilateral attempt to change it.

Berlin represents part of a larger issue — the ultimate reunification of Germany. The Russians are dead set against it, emphasis on dead; they lost more than 20 million people — men, women, and children — at the hands of the Nazis. They have long memories. Truth be told, the rest of the Europeans aren't too crazy about the idea, either. Americans are noncommittal. The Germans on both sides haven't given up; but for them, the notion of one Germany, whole again, has become a sort of Arcadia, a hazy dream that will be realized someday, if not in this life.

There are the neutrals: Austria leans firmly to the West, although it is not a member of NATO and does not want to be. Yugoslavia belongs to no one, not even the Yugoslavians; it is a political artifice, made up of parts left over from World War II. The only thing the various ethnic groups in Yugoslavia have in common is their intense dislike for one another. Tito held them together, but Tito's long gone. Neither the East nor the West is ready to use force to bring Yugoslavia into their camp, but it's a good bet each would be willing to go to war to prevent the other side from doing so. Albania was Communist, then Maoist, and is now slightly to the right of Darth Vader, politically. Who cares? There's nothing in Albania worth fighting for.

The Soviet bloc is not rock-solid. The Soviet Union is the only country in the world surrounded by hostile socialist states. China makes them nervous. Afghanistan won't go away. And then there's always the Warsaw Pact.

The Agreement on Friendship, Coordination, and Mutual Assistance was signed in Warsaw (hence the name Warsaw Pact) in 1955, six years after NATO coalesced in the West. The Russians always point this out, as if the Warsaw Pact was formed as a direct result of the rest of Europe ganging up on them; but the truth is that the formation of NATO signaled just the start of a unified military alliance, whereas the pact forces had existed, in all but name, for years.

In addition to the Soviet Union, there are seven signatories to the Warsaw Pact. Nearly every one has revolted against the Russians at least once (except for Bulgaria, whose enthusiasm for communism verges on embarrassing, even to the Soviets). It's important to remember the non-Soviet Warsaw Pact nations are not the monolith depicted by the governments of both sides. They are, instead, a widely disparate group of proud, formerly sovereign nations who happened to be in the wrong place (Eastern Europe) at the wrong time (World War II).

The U.S. and its Western European allies might have family fights on occasion, but it *is* a family. NATO might as well be the fifty-first state, compared with the undercurrents rippling through the Warsaw Pact: The Hungarians hate the Romanians; the Romanians hate the Hungarians *and* the Bulgarians; the Czechs hate the East Germans; the Poles hate the East Germans; and everybody hates the Russians.

Look at the record — East German riots, Polish labor revolts, Czechoslovakian unrest, Hungarian uprisings, all put down by Soviet forces in no unsubtle fashion, some invasions reluctantly attended by other Warsaw Pact forces to make it look good. This will take its toll. Most Warsaw Pact armies are capable of only limited action, of a defensive nature if that. And in some countries, more Soviet troops will have to be devoted to garrisoning cities and baby-sitting Warsaw Pact forces than the forces those armies contribute.

A closer look at the Warsaw Pact forces reveals a number of surprises. The Polish army still has a chaplain corps. It's possible (although, admittedly, not advisable) to be a conscientious objector in East Germany. Romania refuses to allow forces from any other country — including the Soviet Union — to set foot on its territory, or even cross its borders on the way to somewhere else.

The nature of this uncertain alliance makes predicting World War III a chancy business. There are too many "scenario-dependent" variables, to use the compound word that compounds problems for Pentagon wargamers. Would the Pact armies fight? Whom would they fight? Barring the most provocative moves on the part of NATO, it's cautiously conceded now that any "bolt from the blue" Soviet invasion from garrison would have to be a unilateral one. The East Germans might go along with it, provided they could be convinced an invasion might bring about unification — a nice trick. The Czechs could be nudged, maybe. The rest are probably unwilling or unable to perform any military action short of self-defense.

With the European Pact forces out of the matrix, the odds don't look so good for the Soviets. Certainly, they make invasion less likely. Whether NATO would hang together is less problematic. For such a benign collection of armies to ever be mobilized, the circumstances would have to be so precipitous that not fighting would be virtually out of the question. The problem with NATO is, instead, its mushy command structure, which seeks to placate the various allies and their often-conflicting war-fighting strategies. The allies agree to disagree in peacetime. How they could hammer out concrete plans quickly in the context of a general war is anybody's guess.

So although both sides jockey for position, encourage unrest, and do their best to embarrass each other, in Europe the lines are well drawn and no one steps over them. The greatest danger lies in the peripheral areas, where the roles are not as clearly defined, and with the possibility of a limited confrontation in, say, the Middle East or Africa or anywhere in Asia spilling over into Europe.

Not that it's well known, but a multifront war would probably be a bigger problem for the Soviet Union than the United States. Previous administrations have put forth the image of an awesome Soviet war machine; in truth, the Russians have some real difficulties in mounting and sustaining a general offensive, especially on more than one front. Most of the countless Soviet divisions the U.S. Defense Department likes to publicize are actually shadow units, some at little more than cadre strength, made up of provincial soldiers who receive little training and speak no Russian. Proposed Soviet troop withdrawals in eastern Europe, although impressive sounding, promise to do little more than put real bite behind the remaining divisions.

The Soviet Union is huge, but its production and transportation facilities are not. Supply lines are fairly easily interdicted. The Soviet Union does have oil, but no sure way to get it to the armored units under attack. The troops are routinely mobilized to help get the harvest in; who will carry in the crops when the fighting starts? The Soviets stockpile a lot of weapons, but their style of fighting almost guarantees they will run short very quickly in a general war.

This does not mean the Red Army is hollow. They would be almost unbeatable on the defensive. But NATO has no plans to attack. They couldn't if they wanted to. Except for, perhaps, the French Army and some USAREUR units, NATO forces are organized for the defense.

What this adds up to is the status quo. Everyone stays put. Except for the fact that it is a tremendous economic and emotional drain on both sides, it is an acceptable situation. One thing that could tip the balance is a ''secret weapon,'' a capability developed by one side that threatens to put the other at a significant disadvantage. The Strategic Defense Initiative — the administration's ''Star Wars'' program — is such a weapon. The Russians are scared to death of it. Neither will the Russians sit still for, say, the development of an independent West German

nuclear capability, or any unilateral unprovoked assault by the United States against Iran, even though there is no love lost between Moscow and Tehran. Destabilization has almost been an act of war in the last half of the twentieth century.

For its part, the United States has staked out its strategic interests. There are many, and most border the Soviet Union: the Persian Gulf, Pakistan, Korea, and the Pacific Rim. Much of its attention is focused on Central America, where the Soviet Union has not dared intervene directly.

These are the likely starting blocks for World War III, not the Luneburg Heath or the Fulda Gap. The Rand Corporation recently did a fascinating, if frightening, study on the future of war. They concluded that armed conflict in the remainder of the twentieth century would be less destructive, but also less coherent. What's going on

''OPFOR'' M60 fires off its smoke-discharging shot simulator. Real opposing forces fire real bullets.

123

now in Lebanon is the model for future wars: operations on three levels — conventional warfare, guerrilla raids, and acts of terrorism — wars among nations, factions, and terrorist campaigns going on simultaneously, using weapons ranging from the latest high-tech military hardware to car bombs, with operations spanning assassinations to combined arms tactics, often in urban environments.

The study concluded that wars, once begun, will never end, because *the causes that limit war also foster and continue it.* These include the increasing cost and lethality of modern weapons, the complex roles of the superpowers, who alternately encourage and discourage hostilities, and the limitations of world and domestic opinion in an age of global communications. These also lead to a greater reliance on unconventional or indirect forms of warfare (terrorists) and the use of proxies (mercenaries for the West and Cuban and East European ''advisers'' for the Soviet bloc).

The Rand study contained these chilling thoughts: ''Warfare will cease to be finite. The distinction between war and peace will dissolve. With constraints on the use of military force, wars will seldom end in conquest or capitulation. Cease-fires will be imposed by external powers, or occur because the belligerents temporarily exhaust themselves or are unwilling to face the risks of escalation. The losers will consider their defeats temporary. Implacable foes will fight repeated wars. Nominal peace will be filled with confrontations and crises. National boundaries will be blurred. Refugees will carry the seeds of war with them. Hostilities will be endless.''

This is truly scary, and not at all like the image of World War III we've been reading about: Europe once again in flames. Helicopters whopping over a ridge line, some blooming into red balls and black smoke, others spitting bright rockets that ring into the advancing armor. Overhead, jets stitch white vapor trails in the blue sky. That's how we fight World War III on the book racks. Different versions, all with the same ending. *A near thing!*

So let's leave the tanks where they are, muzzle to muzzle, until dust settles over their armor and, like the Hapsburg knights, they are seen as quaint but impressive anachronisms. It's Strauss this time, not Wagner, and all's quiet on the Western Front.

This typical Bavarian town carries on its daily business caught between the most formidable armies the world has ever known.

Left: Like all Hawk sites in West Germany, this battery belongs to the 32d ADCOM. The sites are manned and ready 24 hours a day.

Appendix

USAREUR CAMOUFLAGE AND MARKINGS

Never the most colorful of services, the U.S. Army has gotten even more drab in recent years. Although some vehicles may sport colorful — and unofficial — nicknames and markings, the official goal is to have vehicles blend in, not stand out. The purpose, of course, is camouflage, to keep the other guy from seeing you before you see him. In addition, projecting a low heat signature is vital today, especially at night, when so many night vision devices depend at least partially on infrared for detection. Consequently, the Army's newest finishes for armored fighting vehicles have the now common shimmer of infrared suppressive paint.

Just as the Army wasted much time tinkering with tank design before settling on the M1, it went through quite a few color combinations before arriving — or not arriving — at a consistent, USAREUR-wide camouflage finish for tanks and infantry fighting vehicles. The U.S. Army has never been big on sophisticated camouflage schemes. In the beginning, anything that moved was painted olive drab (except for things that moved on sand, which were sand-colored). This system worked effectively from the end of World War II to about ten years ago (but then, all camouflage finishes are effective in peacetime).

The Army once tried a strange "digitized" scheme called "Dualtex," in which contrasting camouflage colors were applied upon an olive drab base in small, square bits. The cubic camouflage, while potentially cheap and versatile, was too weird to be taken seriously — troops felt *more,* not less, conspicuous running around in "polka-dot" tanks.

Dualtex was replaced by a camouflage "system" developed by the Army's Mobility Equipment Research and Development Command (MERDC). Using about a dozen standard colors, AFVs could be painted to blend in with just about any type of terrain on earth. Moreover, just by changing one or two of the colors in a typical four-color MERDC pattern, a tank's camouflage could change with the seasons.

Like most Army notions of the 1970s, it was a good idea on paper, but came up short in the field. In order to work, the MERDC patterns had to be applied a great deal more carefully than soldiers in the motor pool were willing or capable. And the idea of repainting a tank that didn't need it just because the leaves were falling fell on deaf ears in an army hard pressed to keep up with even basic maintenance.

Consequently, most of the new M1s and M2s, which were delivered to USAREUR in their factory finish of overall forest green, stayed that way. In most photographs, USAREUR armor appears gray, not green; this is because the majority of pictures are shot at ranges, where generations of tanks have churned the earth and gravel into a fine, concrete-colored mist that settles over everything.

Perhaps it's just as well, because the West Germans had their own ideas about how tanks should be camouflaged. The Bundeswehr pushed for a common camouflage system for all NATO AFVs. It would make it more difficult for an enemy to distinguish the nationality of a tank just from its camouflage (in the case of countries that use the same design, such as the Leopard),

or the type of tank and therefore its origin (in cases like the M1, used only by the U.S.). More important, the enemy would find it more difficult to exploit seams in the defenses, where units from different nations overlap, just by watching the tanks change colors.

Although MERDC's four-color camouflage was marginally more effective than the German three-color, the Bundeswehr is the unquestioned backbone of NATO's land forces. So in the summer of 1988, MERDC suddenly announced it had come up with new "three-color camouflage

Bumper codes identify this M3 as belonging to V Corps, 3d Squadron, 11th ACR, L Troop, 1st platoon, commander's vehicle.

patterns for all tactical equipment, replacing a less-effective four-color scheme used previously," and that "the German Army, which cooperated with the concept, is now repainting its equipment and other NATO countries are considering the three-color pattern." The new scheme of two greens and a black will probably be applied to vehicles at the factory.

There really is nothing else on American tanks but camouflage paint. Those big white stars from World War II are long gone, replaced by black stars that gradually shrank and disappeared. There are the usual warnings and bridge-weight class stencils, all in low-viz black. And recently armor and mech infantry units have adopted a code system for distinguishing friendly units.

The system, which varies with the unit, uses geometric shapes and colors mounted on a panel on the rear of the turret or on the commander's hatch. These markings are easily seen and are a great help on the range, but it's a sure bet the crews would not wear them to a war. More permanent are the bumper codes, which, reading right to left, denote the parent division, regiment, battalion, company, and vehicle number.

THE 32ND ADCOM

USAREUR's 32nd ADCOM is the largest air defense command in the world. It "owns" all American theater-level antiaircraft assets in Europe, including Hawk and new Patriot surface-to-air missile sites (but not the short-ranged Vulcan, Chapparal, and Stinger systems, which are organic to the divisions). Because of its size and scope, 32nd ADCOM, while definitely subordinate to USAREUR, is, in effect, a separate, pervasive entity, protecting all of southern Germany under its antiair umbrella.

Like the rest of USAREUR, 32nd ADCOM has gone through some changes recently. A decade ago all the missiles were lined up in a "Hawk Belt" that, along with Hawks from other NATO countries, stretched north to south across West Germany, border to border. With the introduction of Patriot — a truly formidable, if scarce, system — the Hawk Belt has been unbuckled and the NATO SAMs scattered across Germany in a more comprehensive system. We are told they protect "selected, high-value locations," but the Army has gotten a lot more closed-mouthed about SAM deployments in recent years.

Hawk sites are invariably placed on desolate, windswept hilltops. The sites are identified by an alphanumeric — "Echo 182," for example — but informally and more typically they are named after the town nearest their home site.

A typical Hawk battery will actually have two or three alternate sites where it deploys for exercises and alerts, and many more surveyed for actual wartime. Hawk batteries used to be "square" — with four separate firing units — then "triad," and are now "biad," with two platoons.

There are no more self-propelled Hawk launchers in Europe; it was counterproductive to put the things on tracks in the first place, since the parade of associated equipment necessary to make it work had to be hauled around by truck, including the big control vans that are the "heart and brains of the operation," according to a battery commander.

If the sites are "active" — loaded and ready to launch, as most of them are — they pull what is called a NATO state of alert. While in "NATO State" the sites are incorporated into NADGE, the NATO Air Defense Ground Environment.

"We are, at peace and at war, under NATO operational control," says a Hawk battery commander. "We are under NATO command right now. My orders come from battalion TOC, the tactical operations center. They get theirs from brigade or SOC — sector operations center — the multinational command center run by NATO.''

But in wartime SOC and TOC and all the other command echelons are likely to be incommunicado, at best. Then it's up to the tactical control officer in the command van with the trigger at the end of a long coiled cord to fire or not to fire. How do they know if that target — D12, for example — is friend or foe?

"We have certain rules of engagement we go by. It's all standard NATO doctrine that determines who's the good guy, who's the bad guy, who we can fire on.

"There are procedural rules during wartime — certain altitudes, certain airspeeds, being in a certain corridor — that tends to make him friendly. But the rules would change all the time."

You know what they say about Army rules, though: There's always some poor sucker who doesn't get the word. In one test of the airspace management plan, the only players who seemed to get with the program were East German MiG pilots, who mockingly mirrored the supposedly secret altitude and airspeed requirements on their side of the border.

Hawk dog! Sam the battery pooch protects the geese that protect the missiles that protect the forces that protect our freedom.

The Author

Michael Skinner has been a writer and editor for the *St. Petersburg Times,* the *Washington Star,* and Cable News Network. He is the author of USAFE: A PRIMER OF MODERN AIR COMBAT IN EUROPE, RED FLAG: AIR COMBAT FOR THE '80s (Presidio AIRPOWER books), and USN: NAVAL OPERATIONS IN THE '80s. Skinner is currently at work on a novel.